Blacks and Criminal Justice

Blacks and Criminal Justice

Edited by
Charles E. Owens
University of Alabama

Jimmy Bell
Jackson State University

Lexington Books
D.C. Heath and Company
Lexington, Massachusetts
Toronto

Library of Congress Cataloging in Publication Data

Main entry under title:
    Blacks and criminal justice.

    Includes index.
    1. Criminal justice, Administration of—United States—Addresses,
essays, lectures. 2. Afro-Americans—Addresses, essays, lectures. 3. Afro-
American criminals—Addresses, essays, lectures. 4. Education of pris-
oners—United States—Addresses, essays, lectures. I. Owens, Charles E.
II. Bell, Jimmy.
HV8138.B53   364'.973   76-43639
ISBN 0-669-01101-0

utbs 16.00/14.40 /3/31/80

Second printing, December 1978

Published simultaneously in Canada

Printed in the United States of America

International Standard Book Number: 0-669-01101-0

Library of Congress Catalog Card Number: 76-43639

To Otis and Clara
Bryant, Chris, Chuck, Arlinda, Meredith,
Rasheda and Sonya

Contents

Foreword   ix

Preface   xi

Part I An Overview   1

Chapter 1   **What Price Justice: An Introduction**
Charles E. Owens   3

Chapter 2   **Looking Back Black** *Charles E. Owens*   7

Chapter 3   **Blacks and Criminal Justice Today**
Richard W. Velde   17

Chapter 4   **Researching Black Justice: Descriptions and
Implications** *Samuel Barnett*   25

Part II Focus on Equality and Inequality   35

Chapter 5   **Discretionary Justice and the Black Offender**
Taunya Banks   37

Chapter 6   **Challenge for the Judicial System: Economic
and Racial Equality** *George W. Crockett, Jr.*   47

Chapter 7   **Elitism: Perpetuation Through Incarceration**
Laurence French   53

Part III Black Crime: Offenders and Victims   67

Chapter 8   **Crime in the Black Community** *Jimmy Bell*
and *Irv Joyner*   69

Chapter 9   **Rape, Race, and Research** *Patricia Evans*   75

Chapter 10   **Black Women: Income and Incarceration**
Eleanor Saunders Wyrick and *Otis Holloway Owens*   85

Part IV Answers and Actions   93

Chapter 11   **Prison Education: Perspectives Past and Present**
                     C. Schweber-Koren   95

Chapter 12   **Higher Education: Roles in Criminal Justice**
                     Jimmy Bell   113

Chapter 13   **Improving Police Relations in the Black Community**
                     L. Alex Swan   119

Chapter 14   **Classifying Black Inmates: The Alabama Prison**
                     Classification Project   *Charles E. Owens*   129

Chapter 15   **Summary**   *Charles E. Owens* and *Jimmy Bell*   143

                     Index   145

                     List of Contributors   153

                     About the Editors   155

Foreword

Webster's New World Dictionary defines justice as "1. a being right; 2. fairness; 3. a being correct; 4. sound reason, rightfulness; 5. reward or penalty as deserved; 6. the use of authority to uphold what is right, just, lawful; 7. *the administration of law*" [italics added]. Unfortunately for most blacks who find themselves involved in the American criminal justice system, either as offenders or as victims, it is the seventh definition of justice that is applied: "the administration of law." If, indeed, justice to blacks does mean "the administration of law" this book could appropriately be titled *Blacks and the Administration of Law in Criminal Cases*. The articles in this book are addressed to the administration of criminal laws as they are applied to blacks.

 Blacks and Criminal Justice shares with its readers articles written by many persons who have had direct contact with the American criminal justice system. Contributors range from persons who are ingrained in and a part of the system to activitists who shout for change, to governmental officials who recognize that justice is not administered equally to blacks, to scholars who have extensive training in behavioral sciences and are full of suggestions for change. The purpose of this book is to share the ideas of its contributors, and to inform and sensitize its readers to the realities of our criminal justice system.

 To those readers who are somewhat familiar with our present system of criminal justice: there are articles which may give documentation to your worst fears about the system.

 To those readers who are totally ignorant of the workings of our great system of criminal justice: you are in for some surprises.

One who has been there.

Sue Thompson, J.D.
Member, Alabama Prisons
Human Rights Committee

Preface

The theme of this book, blacks and the criminal justice system, reflects the deeply rooted and growing concern of the American public. The relationship between black American citizens and the criminal justice system is multi-faceted and highly complex. There is a critical need to identify, to interpret, and to clarify the subtle nuances of this relationship.

The University of Alabama through its Department of Psychology Center for Correctional Psychology sponsored two separate conferences (1974 and 1975) which sought to provide a forum for examining and elucidating the underlying causes and effects of the theme: blacks and the criminal justice system. These two conferences were attended by over 1,000 persons from thirty-eight states and included attorneys, college students, community organizers, correctional officers, judges, law enforcement officers, mental health professionals, medical personnel, parole board members, prison guards, public officials, and other interested persons.

There were two highly significant outcomes of these conferences. First, the idea for writing this book was formed. The conferences clearly showed that there was not enough printed information available to the broad-based constituency reflected by the conference attendees. Further, the dearth of material which discussed the criminal justice system with the black experience as a frame of reference was inhibiting to those persons who prepared and presented papers. Some of the articles, rewritten for this publication, were originally given as papers at the conferences on blacks in the criminal justice system.

The second outcome was the birth of the National Association of Blacks in Criminal Justice (NABCJ). This organization continues to address the issues and concerns of blacks and the criminal justice system and to represent the wide range of people who work within and are affected by the tenuous relationship between blacks and the criminal justice system.

Those individuals who helped to make the writing of this book a reality are gratefully acknowledged. Inspiration was received from countless friends associates, and fellow members of NABCJ. Colleagues in the University of Alabama Department of Psychology, especially Stanley Brodsky, were both encouraging and supportive.

Gail Morgan ably assisted in the final preparation of the materials.

Otis Holloway Owens, an unusual muse, worked diligently throughout the writing of this book and generously provided constructive feedback and special assistance.

Part I

An Overview

1

What Price Justice:
An Introduction

Charles E. Owens

An American Negro folktale titled, "A Fine for Killing Two Negroes" (Dorson, 1967), represents the central dilemma of blacks in the American justice system. The story tells of an old black man and his two sons; a white fellow, named Willie; and a mule. The old man and his two sons, who had the reputation of being as bad as they could be, rode into town on their mules. They were after Willie who had whipped one of the sons the previous day. The old man fired a shot at Willie and missed. Willie, in turn, fired and killed the old man and one of the sons. The second son hid behind the mule. Again, Willie shot, killing the mule. Willie was taken to court, tried and fined five dollars for killing the mule and a nickel for killing the two black men.

This folktale aptly accentuates one of the main concerns that blacks have had and continue to have about the criminal justice system: the seemingly low value placed on the black person. What is the price of justice for blacks, either as offenders or as victims?

The writing of this book was prompted by a need to bring to the forefront the concern for the price blacks must pay for justice. In addition, other issues and injustices of the criminal justice process related to the black experience must be examined. The goals of this book are to provide an understanding of the interfacing of blacks and the system of justice and to present to the reader alternatives and recommendations for dealing with a system that has been unjust to many blacks.

The criminal justice system may be defined as the process of interlocking functions designed to prevent and control crime, to provide a procedure for moving persons from phase to phase within the process, and to rehabilitate offenders. While there are, of course, many similarities among law violators, involvement in the criminal justice process has been distinctly different for black Americans. Historically, justice has been Janus-faced. The criminal justice system has been used to protect the white and rich and to control the black and poor.

The ideal criminal justice system would have the following characteristics: it would not discriminate against a person because of color or class; it would minimize further penetration into the system; and it would provide adequate rehabilitational services at each level.

To date, the system has failed to respond effectively in providing rehabilitative techniques for blacks. Until rehabilitative and diversionary programs can influence black offenders, the already overcrowded jails and prisons will

3

continue to be filled disproportionately with this population. If the price for killing two black men increased to fifty cents, some might consider this to be progress. However, if the price of the mule also increased in value, to fifty dollars, others would know that nothing has really changed.

The selections in this book have been written by professionals who represent a cross-section of fields and levels within the criminal justice system. The selections are designed to appeal to audiences from many segments of society including decisionmakers, law enforcement personnel, program planners, and others who have either a connection to or an interest in justice. It is meant especially to be a resource book for those who teach and study criminal justice courses.

Chapter 2, "Looking Back Black," traces the historical relationship of blacks and the criminal justice system from the arrival of African slaves in colonial America to the present. Accordingly, Charles E. Owens tells that the experience of blacks with justice can be categorized by two periods. The first, Plantation Justice (1600s to 1865), was maintained through the slave codes, the Constitution (Article 1, Section 2), the Dred Scott Decision, and lynching and other terrorist tactics.

The period of criminal justice (i.e., justice that is criminal), ushered in by the end of the Civil War, the Emancipation Proclamation, and the Thirteenth Amendment to the Constitution, was nurtured by the Black Codes, the crop lien or sharecropping system, the Ku Klux Klan, lynchings, legal executions, the court processes, and other atrocities.

Richard W. Velde offers a contemporary view of "Blacks and Criminal Justice Today" in Chapter 3. Velde gives a statistical summary of black offenders, victims, employment in criminal justice, and juveniles. Velde presents strategies for change and spells out the limitations of the Law Enforcement Assistance Administration (LEAA) and other corrections agencies in solving the nation's social problems of alienation, family disintegration, poverty, lack of education, drugs, disease, and mental aberrations.

Chapter 4 reviews the portrayal of the black offender in "Researching Black Justice: Descriptions and Implications." Samuel Barnett examines five selected areas including police and arrests, the courts, black judges and attorneys, prisons, and parole and probation. Barnett states that generally, blacks have been presented in a negative posture with little attention being paid to the psychological struggle of the black offender. More empirical data on the black offender is obviously needed.

The use of discretionary powers by the American justice system has been institutionalized. Two authors, Taunya Banks and George Crockett, express differing views of how the whole arena of discretion can be applied.

In "Discretionary Justice and the Black Offender" (Chapter 5), Banks points out how the use of discretion in the administration of justice has resulted in the discrimination and oppression of blacks. She advocates the application of more rigid guidelines and the elinination of broad-based discretion in administrative action by police departments, prosecuting officers, and courts so that blacks can experience equity and parity within the system.

Crockett attributes the evils of the criminal justice system not to race but to class. Chapter 6, "Challenge for the Judicial System: Economic and Racial Equality," reveals that historically the judicial system has served as a refuge for the oppressed from the discriminatory actions of the two branches of government. Crockett concludes that the judge at the apex of the judicial system, when dedicated, can use discretions constructively to produce change in how the judiciary responds to blacks and poor people.

Chapter 7, "Elitism: Perpetuation Through Incarceration," by Lawrence French, articulates the dramatic manner in which incarceration has been used to perpetuate the power of the elites over other segments of the American society. Deviance, rather than being an absolute, is defined by the dominant elites in a manner which reinforces their boundaries. French focuses on the North Carolina Prison System to illustrate this point.

A stimulating account of "Crime in the Black Community" is presented by Irv Joyner and Jimmy Bell in Chapter 8. These authors probe the effects of deprivation in the face of wealth and the resulting criminal activities of the black offender. Joyner and Bell list strategies and techniques to be employed by blacks in resisting and controlling crime in their communities.

There are two chapters centered on concerns of women. In "Rape, Race, and Research" (Chapter 9), Patricia Evans examines the misinformation, misunderstanding, and misconceptions surrounding this crime committed by men against women. Evans discusses interracial rape as the two-edged sword for blacks. The black male, as rapist, has been severely punished, lynched, or legally executed for proven or alleged rapes of white females. In contrast, when a black female is raped by a white male, the rapist is not likely to be punished as harshly.

Eleanor Saunders Wyrick and Otis Holloway Owens show the interrelationship of "Black Women: Income and Incarceration" in Chapter 10. These authors report that too often correctional rehabilitation and education programs train women for the lowest paying jobs, thereby fastening the black incarcerated female to an economic carousel. They offer increasing the representation of women in the correctional work force as one solution for this situation.

Chapter 11, "Prison Education: Perspectives Past and Present," by C. Schweber-Koren, summarizes an exhaustive investigation of prison education in federal correctional institutions. Schweber-Koren details the historical background of correctional education, looks at the educational characteristics of black federal prisoners, evaluates the current educational programs, and poses provocative questions for further research.

In "Higher Education: Roles in Criminal Justice" (Chapter 12), Jimmy Bell discusses the need for higher education to address the problems blacks

encounter with crime and the criminal justice system. He contends higher education can contribute to amelioration through research; training and recruiting
students in law, criminal justice, and correctional psychology; providing post-
secondary opportunities for inmates; and direct involvement in the system.

Alex Swan presents a paradigm for "Improving Police Relations in the
Black Community" in Chapter 13. Swan explains that community residents
must assume the initiative in defining and establishing police-community relations. In Swan's schema, community residents would provide input in the
establishment of programs, policies, priorities, the resolution of disputes, and
the employment and dismissal of police.

Chapter 14 focuses on "Classifying Black Inmates: The Alabama Prison
Classification Project." Written as a result of Charles Owens' participation in
the project, it addresses the issues of how subtleties of racism can be manifested
in the classification process through the abuses of testing, subjective decision-
making, gut level feelings, and therapeutic referrals.

The chapters may be read in sequence or individually. Any or all chapters
will provide the reader with an in-depth understanding of the problems, of no
small proportions, which blacks have historically encountered and continue to
encounter in their relations with and passage through the system. The complexity of finding solutions for making this truly a system of justice for blacks
is exceeded only by the complexity of the dynamics of the system. Nevertheless, these authors have optimistically offered suggestions based on close-range
observation and examinations.

Reference

Dorson, Richard. *American Negro Folktales.* Greenwich, Conn.: Fawcett Pub-
    lications, 1967.

2

Looking Back Black

Charles E. Owens

The criminal justice system is the operative arm of government created for the purpose of apprehending, adjudicating, and incarcerating those who violate the laws of society. It has been charged with the responsibility of administering justice in an impersonal and unbiased manner. History, however, has demonstrated quite convincingly that the justice dispensed in America is not blind, unbiased, or impersonal. It has been a dual justice system; as a result black and poor people have been disproportionately represented as clients in this system. Perhaps the best way to influence or change the criminal justice system would be for all poor and black people to refuse to commit crimes. This oversimplified statement acknowledges the fact that blacks are so important to the maintenance of the justice system that the system would collapse if blacks were removed or prevented from entering. The black person has not been spared contact at any level with representatives of the criminal justice system, including the police, the courts, and the correctional system.

In order to understand why this parasitic condition exists, it is important to realize that all of the present attitudes and many of the current criminal justice policies are so deeply interwoven in America's early slave system that the justice system of today is in many respects only an extension and manifestation of this earlier system. The treatment that blacks have received is in no way contradictory to the basic philosophical foundation of either system.

Plantation Justice

In order to understand the precarious relationship that now exists between the criminal justice apparatus and the black man, it is necessary to look back at the roots of this phenomenon, the plantation. The dual system of justice was conceived when the first black person was imported to the shores of America as a slave. From the beginning, blacks were not meant to receive equal justice with the white man. As a result of their color and economic status, blacks were subjected to a unique form of justice. This early system of justice could appropriately be called *plantation justice*, for it was on the plantation where the power of justice and injustice was invested. The slave codes of 1690 were the earliest written attempt to define how plantation justice was administered. These codes, a group of laws designed specifically for the discipline and control of the slave, clearly delineated the social and legal relationship of the black man to the white

7

man. Even though the codes were not consistent from colony to colony, they
all were generally designed to prevent slaves from carrying weapons, owning
property, and having rights or legal protection. Blacks, for example, could not
testify in court, serve on juries, make contracts, sell goods, leave the plantation
without a ticket from the master or a representative, use insulting language
toward whites, or strike a white person (Meier and Rudwick, 1970).

As long as the black man was not considered equal to the white man, there
was no need to be concerned with equal justice and treatment. Therefore, punishments for disobeying the codes were severe and generally unrestrictive. Whatever the mind could conjure up could be used and justified as appropriate
justice: branding, lashing, ear cropping, hanging, whipping, dismemberment,
and burnings were examples of punishments used during this period. The ultimate punishment, death, was meted out for rape or attempted rape of a white
woman, murder or attempted murder, revolt or attempted revolt, robbery, and
in some instances, striking a white person. The dealth penalty, however, was
usually enforced against slaves only when whites were the victims.

In order to enforce the codes during the period of slavery, any and all
white men were automatically given license to challenge any black person, to
bear arms against any black man, and to apprehend any black who was unable
to present a satisfactory explanation of why he was out by himself. In fact, in
highly populated slave areas, white men were required to serve on slave patrols,
which were to protect the community during nonworking hours (Jordan, 1973).
While these punishments and control methods were stringent, they were reflective of the negative image of the black man.

The Constitution of the United States did not help to offset the image.
Indeed, it can be said that the Constitution helped to nourish the climate for
the treatment of slaves. Article 1, Section 2, Paragraph 3 of the United States
Constitution considered each black slave equal to three-fifths of a human being.
This, then, was the environment in which the black slave received justice until
December 18, 1865, when the Thirteenth Amendment abolishing slavery was
ratified.

While the slave status was undesirable, being a freed black man still did not
insulate the black man from abuse nor provide him with equal rights. The freed
black man was still subjected to a different standard of justice from the white
man. Jordan (1973) suggests that some colonists perceived the freed black man
(which implied that he was not controlled) as a greater threat to their well-being
than the slave population. Therefore, laws and regulations were passed which
controlled and restricted the rights and privileges of the free black man. In the
District of Columbia and Ohio, they were required to post bond to guarantee
their good behavior and to report to the police at regular intervals; they could
not testify against whites in court in Indiana, California, and Virginia; they were
required to have a sponsor for carrying guns in South Carolina; and if they did
not have visible means of support in Maryland, they were required to post bond,

leave the state, or be sentenced to six months servitude (Jordan, 1973; Meier and Rudwick, 1970; Froman, 1972). The Dred Scott Decision cemented the black man's "less than human status." This landmark decision defined the relationship between American black and white men. Blacks were further removed from any type of equal justice by the acclamation that the Negro had no rights which the white man needed to respect (Lincoln, 1969).

From 1619 until the Civil War, the scenario was set and the foundation was laid for the subsequent role and relationships the blacks would develop and maintain with the criminal justice system. The discriminatory justice had its genesis during this period of American history. Any subsequent treatment, practices, and policies were either an exacerbation or a proliferation of the practices and policies of the slave system. The discriminatory practices within criminal justice today were part of this system: unequal protection in the courts, excessive and inhumane punishment, poor medical attention, inadequate diets, severe penalties for blacks when the victim was white, unequal treatment by the police, and unequal representation at all levels of the criminal justice system. The end of the Civil War spawned the hope of both blacks and whites that these injustices would be corrected.

Criminal Justice

The Civil War altered the relationship of the black man to the justice system in numerous ways. The Civil War marked the major point of influx into the penal system for blacks. Prior to the Civil War and the signing of the Emancipation Proclamation, black slaves were not considered legally responsible for criminal acts except for special cases such as insurrection or murder of a white person, and in these cases the penalty was usually death. Other infractions were punished by the master under the plantation justice system. After the signing of the Emancipation Proclamation, however, blacks were no longer considered slaves and were, in fact, held legally responsible for all criminal acts. The Thirteenth Amendment, ratified in 1865, abolished slavery and was written in language that signaled a new interactional pattern between blacks and the justice system. Section 1 said:

Neither slavery nor involuntary servitude except as a punishment for crime whereof the party shall have been duly convicted, shall exist within the U.S. or any place subject to their jurisdiction . . . .

The Thirteenth Amendment changed the relationship from plantation justice to criminal justice. The subtle language of this law gave credence to and legitimized what was to happen to black people for the next one hundred years. It said a slave system could still be maintained as long as legal ways were found to make sure that the black man was "duly convicted." This was accomplished very skillfully by the creation of clever and insidious arrangements and laws which helped to increase the number of black convicted felons. The "Black Codes," created by Mississippi in 1865, were eventually adopted throughout the South (Meier and Rudwick, 1970). Under these codes, blacks who were unemployed or without a permanent residence were declared vagrants and could be arrested and fined; if unable to pay the fine, they were rented out for labor.

The crop lien system or sharecropping system, was another technique used to keep the black man in servitude. Originally, sharecropping was designed as a fair and equitable arrangement. The black man rented land from the white man and planted the crops; both parties shared the profits from the sale of the crops. The system, however, eventually became an albatross for many blacks. The slave system had left many of the blacks illiterate or semiliterate, and many were afraid to assert their rights. Some landowners capitalized on this apparent weakness and charged inflated prices for materials usually owned by the landowner. After the crop was sold and the books balanced, blacks were likely to end up in debt. The poor black croppers, unable to repay their debts from one year to another, were taken before the law. As a result, they were required either to work for the same dishonest planter to repay the debt for an indefinite period of time or to be incarcerated (Lincoln, 1969). This practice, along with vagrancy laws, provided an inexpensive labor force, affected principally the newly freed southern black population, amounted to only slight modifications of slavery, and insured the continued representation of blacks in the prison system.

Prisons

Incarceration in America's early prisons was an excessively debilitating experience. There was no attempt to disguise the real purpose of the first prisons in our society; they were established as institutions to punish convicted criminals. One of the main components of punishment was hard labor and the financial exploitation of prisoner's manpower.

The convict lease system is one example of how prisoners were exploited. The states rented out prisoners to profit-making corporations, including public and private industries, the railroads, mines, fertilizer plants, and quarries. The convict lease system was typically a very unpleasant experience for the prisoners. Reports revealed that living conditions for the convicts included long working hours, little food, high mortality rates, and rampant disease (Sanborn, 1904).

In order to provide sufficient manpower for the profitable convict lease system, a large prison population was needed. By 1870, there were 8,056 black prisoners in the United States, which comprised about one-third of all prisoners. In 1880, there were 16,000 black prisoners, forming about 40 percent of the total prison population. By 1890, there were 25,000 black inmates again comprising some 40 percent of the total prison population with the greatest number of black prisoners incarcerated in the southern region of the United States (Sanborn, 1904). During the 1930s, Von Hentig (1940) found that black felony convictions were roughly three times the white conviction rates. The U.S. Bureau of Census (U.S. Department of Commerce, 1939) revealed that 44 percent of the prison population was black in 1939.

A punitive and oppressive philosophy, predominant in the prisons, was reflected through rigid repression and regimentation, silence rules, severe punishments, poor and insufficient food, and confinement in small, unsanitary cells that were generally separated from the white prisoners. Until the middle of the twentieth century, black inmates accepted their confinement and punishment in prisons without too much united resistance against the system. Even the courts had a hands-off policy with respect to penal conditions and issues. The conditions and treatment in prison, although considered inhumane and oppressive; the location of prisons, mostly rural; and the composition of the guards, all white; were merely consequences of being black and being criminal.

Enforcement and Control

Founded in 1865, the Ku Klux Klan was a natural outgrowth and extension of the power that the white man used to control the black man during slavery. The Ku Klux Klan eventually evolved into an organized effort to systematically seek out and control blacks who dared to challenge the white man's authority. By 1918, there were several thousand KKK members. The terror that was perpetrated by this group in the black communities and the infamous acts committed have been well documented. The power that they felt and wielded was simply an extension of the early slave patrols. According to Chalmers (1965), the KKK viewed itself as a self-appointed police organization which was the enforcer, not the breaker, of the law and functioned as the police, judiciary, and executioner.

While the KKK was extralegal, the police force was a legitimate agent of the criminal justice system. The police have been the component of the criminal justice system most visibly abrasive to the black man. The non-black population has generally experienced an amiable relationship with the law enforcement component, while the relationship between the black man and the police force in America has historically been severely strained. Gunnar Myrdal (1944) revealed in a classic study that between 1920 and 1932, white officers killed an alarming 54 percent of the 749 blacks killed by white persons in the south and 68 percent outside of the south. From 1930 through the sixties, the continuous use of extensive force and the abuse of power with the black population has continued. Amost every major riot involving blacks in the United States can probably be attributed to some precipitating police action.

The fear of death through the guise of justice, either KKK justice or criminal justice, has been a real and ever present reality to the black man both during and after slavery. The disproportionate number of blacks who were lynched or who received the death penalty reflects the seriousness of these events for blacks. Lynching records maintained by Tuskegee Institute's Department of Records and Research revealed that blacks comprised 72 percent or 3,442 of the 4,736 lynchings during the period from 1882 to 1962. Not only was the act of lynching fatal to the individual, but it was humiliating and emasculating to those blacks who remained, clearly showing that they were vulnerable to this capricious act by white men. It also highlighted their lack of legal protection in American society. Lynching blacks for the slightest infraction served to maintain the black race in a position of powerlessness. At least eighty-five recorded lynching cases were precipitated by insulting language to a white person or conduct considered to be against the mores of a white society, not capital punishment crimes.

The legal execution of prisoners in America reflected a similar trend. Out of a total of 3,859 legal executions in the United States, 53 percent were blacks (U.S. Department of Justice, 1974). Some of the crimes for which blacks were sentenced to death are, at best, of questionable interpretation. It is interesting to note that Nash (1975) wrote two books in which he listed and described the "most notorious outlaws, thieves, brothel keepers, syndicate gangsters, arsonists, rapists, kidnappers, murderers, lovers, forgers, embezzlers, bombers, assassins, bank robbers, and hijackers who have punctuated our history with crime." However, none of these offenders were described as being of purely black origin. Nash's books included the most infamous personalities in the twentieth century up to and including convicted mass murderer Charles Manson, which tends to suggest that although blacks received the death penalty more often than whites, the crimes that blacks were sentenced to death for were not of a magnitude sufficient enough to qualify them as the most serious law breakers in our society.

Courts

Through the court process the individual is brought before the public and judicial system. Even though the role played by the judicial system in the justice process has not been as overtly dehumanizing as the law enforcement and correctional systems, it has been psychologically humiliating to the black man. In addition to the very noticeable discrepancies in sentencing, Downie (1971) noted that blacks have been subjected to verbal abuses and insulting language by judges in the courts. Thus blacks were further entrenched in a position of powerlessness.

The court process also allows for a person to be tried by a jury of peers. Primarily as a carry-over from the slave system, however, blacks were denied full citizenship in the court process. They were restricted from participating in the jury process until 1875, when it was considered illegal by the federal courts to exclude blacks from jury duty because of race. However, the exclusion continued in various forms into the twentieth century. States were known to require prospective jurors to own personal property, to be in respected civic organizations, to be registered voters on poll tax rolls, or to be listed in telephone directories. Some even required certain acceptable personality characteristics (Morgan, 1972; Overby, 1972). For many years, black offenders have generally been tried in the courts by an all white system.

Protest and Riots

The early 1950s ushered in a new relationship with the system—the civil rights or protest movement. It represented a united challenge to the criminal justice system in order to achieve a dream of equality for all men. Scores of blacks and many whites became criminals because of their participation in civil rights activities. Most of the black leaders spent some time in jails or prisons—Martin Luther King, Jr., Stokely Carmichael, Medgar Evers, Ralph Abernathy, Malcolm X, H. Rap Brown, Huey Newton, Angela Davis, and many more. So many blacks spent time in jail that it almost appeared that a black man had to prove his manhood by being imprisoned.

The same courage of the civil rights activists seemed to spill over to prisoners as reflected in the increasing number of prison riots at the midpoint of the twentieth century. Riots or disturbances within the prison system by inmates to protest prison conditions had their most public and sustained beginning about 1952 with the Michigan uprising at Jackson Prison. Since then, almost every penal institution has experienced some type of inmate riot or uprising expressing dissatisfaction with prison conditions (American Correctional Association, 1970). Typical demands presented by prisoners were for better food, removal of unpopular personnel, better medical treatment, less severe disciplinary practices, and better parole systems. It was estimated that blacks participated in almost every riot and in a great many instances were either leaders or co-leaders of the revolt. The bloodiest and most publicized riot was in Attica Prison in New York in 1971 where a total of forty-three people were killed. Of these, thirty-two were inmates and eleven were hostages. Eighty-five inmates and thirty-three correctional employees were wounded (Wicker, 1975). In many respects, the riots only served to vividly illustrate that nothing much had changed since the plantation justice period.

"Looking Back Black," then, is reflecting on the results of one hundred years of criminal justice that has produced a degrading process for siphoning a very visible segment of the population through a dehumanizing system of justice. The departure from plantation justice to criminal justice has simply meant a higher level of sophistication with the difference between the two systems being simply one of degree rather than of substance. The results have been the same. Statistics are not available that can adequately explain or show the number of black citizens who have been humiliated and degraded as a result of this system— either directly, by going through the system as an offender, or indirectly by being denied full citizenship in the decision making process.

"Looking Back Black" is looking at a criminal justice system that had its roots implanted in the black population and as such is a black phenomena. Until it can be seen as such, and dealt with on this level, significant change of the system will not occur. The eradication of injustices in the criminal justice system will require more than just a shallow rehabilitative effort or changing the titles of prisoner to resident or guard to correctional officer. Real and significant changes in the system at every level will be resisted because what is being changed is much more than a simple policy or program. The final denominator is the malignant relationship of the black man to the criminal justice system—a relationship that has been developed, nourished, and maintained since slavery.

References

American Correctional Association. *Riots & Disturbances.* Washington, D.C.: American Correctional Association, 1970.

Chalmers, David M. *Hooded Americanism: The First Century of the Ku Klux Klan, 1865-1965.* New York: Doubleday and Company, 1965.

Downie, Leonard, Jr. *Justice Denied.* Baltimore, Md.: Penguin Publishers, 1971.

Froman, Robert. *Racism.* New York: Dell Publishing Co., 1972.

Jordan, Winthrop D. *White Over Black.* Baltimore, Md.: Penguin Books, 1973.

Lincoln, C. Eric. *The Blackamericans.* New York: Bantam Books, 1969.

Meier, August and Rudwick, Elliott. *From Plantation to Ghetto.* New York: Hill and Wang, 1970.

Morgan, Charles Jr. "Segregated Justice." In Charles E. Reasons and Jack L. Kuykendall (eds.), *Race, Crime and Justice.* Pacific Palisades, Calif.: Goodyear Publishing Co., 1972.

Myrdal, Gunnar. *An American Dilemma.* New York: Harper and Brothers Publishers, 1944.

Nash, Jay Robert. *Bloodletters and Badmen.* Book 2, abridged. New York: Warner Paperback Library, 1975.

———. *Bloodletters and Badmen.* Book 3, abridged. New York: Warner Paperback Library, 1975.

Overby, Andrew. "Discrimination in the Administration of Justice." In Charles E. Reasons and Jack L. Kuykendall (eds.), *Race, Crime and Justice.* Pacific Palisades, Calif.: Goodyear Publishing Co., 1972.

Sanborn, Frank B. "The Problem of Crime." In W.E.B. DuBois (ed.), *Some Notes on Negro Crime, Particularly in Georgia.* Atlanta University Publications #9. Atlanta, Ga.: The Atlanta University Press, 1904.

U.S. Department of Commerce, Bureau of the Census. *Prisoners in State and Federal Prisons and Reformatories.* Washington, D.C.: Government Printing Office, 1939.

U.S. Department of Justice, LEAA. "Capital Punishment, 1971-1972," *National Prisoner Statistics Bulletin.* Washington, D.C.: Government Printing Office, 1974.

Von Hentig, H. "Criminality of the Negro," *Journal of Criminal Law and Criminology* 30 (1940):662-680.

Wicker, Tom. *A Time to Die.* New York: Quadrangle, New York Times Book Co., 1975.

3

Blacks and Criminal Justice Today

Richard W. Velde

For black Americans equality simply means getting the same treatment that white persons get. Just as all others demand fair play, blacks, too, expect the full respect of their inalienable rights—rights that the United States Constitution guarantees to all citizens irrespective of their wealth, social class, or race. These marks of freedom transcend mere theoretical significance. They are the heart of the criminal justice process. Today *all* Americans insist upon equal treatment before the law.

Black Offenders

However, black Americans have a special relationship to the law, both as offenders and as victims. Because of American historical and sociological circumstances, blacks have been involved with this country's criminal justice systems out of proportion to their representation in the total population. According to the Federal Bureau of Investigation's Uniform Crime Report for 1975, more than 25 percent of the persons arrested that year for all types of crimes were black, and more than 47 percent of persons arrested for violent crimes were black. The typical arrested black is a young male. The FBI report for 1975 notes that just under 57 percent of all persons arrested that year were less than twenty-five years old and more than 84 percent were male (U.S. Department of Justice, FBI, 1976).

As a consequence of being arrested relatively more frequently than whites, there are relatively more blacks than whites in confinement. According to a Law Enforcement Assistance Administration (LEAA) survey of local jail inmates, 42 percent of all persons locked up in such facilities are black, and almost 65 percent had failed to complete high school (U.S. Department of Justice, 1974b). What is more, 46 percent of the balck jail inmates had been earning less than $2,000 a year when arrested, and another 12 percent had been earning less than $3,000 a year. Similarly, a 1974 LEAA state prison inmate census indicates that about 47 percent of all prisoners were black, and of this total at least 64 percent had failed to complete high school. Of the blacks who were incarcerated,

52 percent were under twenty-five years old and 75 percent were under thirty
years old (U.S. Department of Justice, LEAA, 1976).

Black Victims

The typical crime victim is also black—a young black male, poor, undereducated,
and unskilled. LEAA's first national crime victim survey revealed that black
males are crime victims at a rate of eighty-five per 1,000 persons, compared with
a rate of seventy-four per 1,000 for white males (U.S. Department of Justice,
1975a). The survey revealed that nationally, blacks are also more likely to be
victims of assault, robbery, rape, and burglary. It is noteworthy, too, that black
households have a higher burglary rate than do white homes in all income groups
from the very poor to the higher socioeconomic levels. One LEAA study of
1972 crime victims in Chicago shows that four out of every 1,000 black women
had been raped, eight out of every 1,000 blacks had been robbed and injured
during a crime, and thirty out of every 1,000 blacks had been robbed without
injury (U.S. Department of Justice, 1974a). Other LEAA surveys showed the
same crime victim patterns in thirteen major American cities.
        Oscar Newman, the director of the Institute of Planning and Housing at
New York University, has studied crime prevention through urban design and
has concluded that certain families are especially likely to become crime victims.
The families that are most vulnerable, he states, are poor, are headed by women,
are black or Puerto Rican, are on some type of public assistance, and have a large
percentage of teenage children (U.S. Department of Justice, 1975b). In 1972,
34 percent of all blacks had incomes below the poverty level, compared to just
10 percent of all whites. Families in Chicago with income of less than $3,000
a year are the victims of violent crimes much more often than individuals—blacks
or whites—with higher annual incomes.

Black Employment in Criminal Justice

Blacks have a special relationship to criminal justice not just as offenders and as
victims. They also stand apart in their participation in the system as decision
makers. They are underemployed in all criminal justice professions—as policemen, corrections officials, judges, lawyers, court administrators, probation
officers, planners—in short, in the whole gamut of criminal justice occupations.
        The Michigan and Massachusetts state police forces are both less than 1
percent black. Throughout the nation only 1.5 percent of all state police officers are black. If one includes local departments and takes the country as a
whole, about 6 percent of all law enforcement officers are black, according to
the International Association of Chiefs of Police.

Juveniles

In 1974 Congress enacted the Juvenile Justice and Delinquency Prevention Act, which has given the federal government a new capability within LEAA for directing the national effort to curb juvenile crime and support treatment for juvenile offenders. As this is so serious a problem, it is absolutely essential that local communities themselves turn to all possible self-help sources. Federal money alone is no panacea.

Profound changes are taking place in the lives of America's children and young people. The American family is being rapidly and radically transformed and permeated with a sense of alienation and rootlessness (Bronfenbrenner, 1974). Almost 45 percent of the nation's mothers now work outside the home. Fifty years ago half of the families in Massachusetts included one adult in addition to the parents. Today the figure is just 4 percent. The percentage of children from divorced families is almost twice what it was a decade ago. If present trends continue, one child in every six will lose a parent through divorce by the time he or she is eighteen years old. During 1970, 10 percent of all children under six years old were living in single-parent families with no father in the home. For the black families these trends are even more pronounced. Of all black children, 53 percent live in families below the poverty line, 44 percent have mothers in the labor force, and 30 percent live in single-parent families (Bronfenbrenner, 1974).

It should be carefully noted, however, that just because a child has a working mother or lives in a one-parent home it does not mean that she or he will become a delinquent or a criminal. The research clearly cautions that although delinquency is related to broken homes, it is not a cause and effect relationship. Not all youths from broken homes become delinquents. Jeffrey and Jeffrey

Table 3-1
Percentage of Children Living with Mothers Only

Race and Age of Child	1960	1970	1973
Total under 18	8	12	14
Black under 18	21	31	38
White under 18	6	9	10
Total under 6	7	11	13
Black under 6	19	31	38
White under 6	5	8	8

Source: U.S. Department of Commerce, Bureau of the Census. *Female Family Heads,* Current Population Reports, series p-23, No. 50. Washington, D.C.: Government Printing Office, 1974, p. 14.

(1970) report several studies by Ferguson, Carr-Saunders, and Trenaman which
support this position. The study by Ferguson revealed that 10 percent of the
working mothers had delinquent boys while 12 percent of the nonworking
mothers had delinquent boys.   Thus, this study concluded that whether or not
the mother is employed outside the home is immaterial. Carr-Saunders found
that in cases where the mother was the sole support of the household, 67 percent
of the delinquent and 52 percent of the controls (nondelinquents) had working
mothers. Trenaman showed that 32 percent of the delinquents and 33 percent
of the controls had working mothers. The vast majority of such children never
become involved with crime or the criminal justice system. There are many
unwanted and unsupervised children who are responsible for juvenile crime,
but there is also an increasing amount of serious crime being committed by the
children of wealthy parents or children who come from so-called good homes.
Most black families are familiar with these facts. However, these matters have
either been totally ignored or insufficiently considered by others.

Strategies for Change

Congress created the Law Enforcement Assistance Administration in 1968 and
directed it to provide state and local criminal justice agencies with federal financial aid and technical help of all kinds to improve their services. However, it
is or should be clear to everyone that police, courts, and corrections agencies
cannot solve the nation's social problems. The elimination of alienation, family
disintegration, poverty, lack of education, drug abuse, disease, mental aberrations, and other such social disorders are beyond their competence. Thus, Congress never intended that LEAA would be responsible for supporting more than
the improvement of state and local criminal justice systems.

Nonetheless, it is especially those individuals whom families, employers,
military services, and schools could not help who end up in the criminal justice
system. They represent more than just unpleasant statistics. They must be
taken into account, for otherwise we will fail in the goal of making the system
work better and thereby reducing criminality. The resources that are available
must be utilized efficiently to accomplish these ends.

The ugly spectacles of the Attica, McAlester, and Huntsville prison disorders in the recent past are vivid reminders of our problems and that we des-
perately need to do more to solve them. Many rehabilitation programs, even
though they may have been conscientiously applied, have failed to significantly
reduce recidivism rates, and offenders reappear in the justice system all too
often. The FBI reports that a study of almost 256,000 offenders in its com-
puterized criminal history file who were arrested from 1970 through 1975
revealed that more than 164,000 (64 percent) had been arrested two or more
times (U.S. Department of Justice, FBI, 1976).

Educational opportunities for offenders, those incarcerated as well as those on probation or parole, need to be improved. A national corrections educational and training network should be developed. It is time to create educational programs tailored to individual learning levels and to the needs of particular corrections institutions. These opportunities should exist for offenders throughout the system, including those on parole or in other probationary categories.

It is necessary that carefully controlled, well-designed, thoroughly evaluated experiments in community corrections alternatives be conducted. Most persons convicted of criminal offenses will one day return to the community, and it is essential that better ways be found to make the transition work.

What is particularly necessary is that criminal justice officials reach out to the black communities within their jurisdictions. A continuing dialogue and a mutual understanding is absolutely essential. Efforts in this direction must be increased.

The nation's black communities can accomplish much on their own initiative and they already have. At the same time, they are aware of the need for more services from their local institutions. Throughout the country they have been demanding greater protection, better facilities, and greater consideration for their particular problems. They deserve this and more, and the criminal justice professionals must see to it that they get them.

Citizens must be encouraged both administratively and financially to help themselves. Self-starting local initiatives have a long and honored tradition in this country, and they typify the American way of solving local problems. Criminal justice is an area in which this can be fostered far more than it has been in the past, although there has been some good progress in this direction. In St. Louis there is a citizen-initiated program that is providing aid to crime victims. The program is administered by a volunteer organization with a small paid staff. The crime victim is helped by the local community—in many cases by his or her own neighbors. The program organizes the neighborhood residents to stay in touch with one another and to help each other in times of need.

The program services emphasize helping victims and their families get in touch with public or private agencies for welfare assistance, food stamps, and hospital care. They help get credit payments extended if a victim loses his or her job or a substantial amount of money. They contact employers to get them to hold open victims' jobs. They see to it that victims get time off to get to court and get transportation to courts, hospitals, police stations, and other locations. The programs also help arrange for child care, grocery shopping, and emergency food, clothing, and shelter. They assist victims file insurance claims, relocate their families, and replace stolen or damaged household goods and essential personal property.

An example of how these victim service programs work is the aid given to a woman whose husband was killed by a criminal. A program volunteer went to see the dead man's widow. The woman was feeling depressed. She said she thought she had lost everything. She said her husband's life insurance policy had lapsed. The volunteer insisted that she get the policy out and examine it. It turned out that the policy still had $1,000 in equity.

Another major LEAA concern is encouraging state and local criminal justice agency efforts to insure the fullest compliance with civil rights legislation. LEAA's office of Civil Rights Compliance is responsible for establishing comprehensive procedures and programs for the effective enforcement of the civil rights responsibilities of LEAA financial assistance recipients in accordance with federal law. The office conducts complaint investigations, civil rights compliance reviews, and monitors federally assisted construction project contractors. It supervises several technical assistance contracts designed to further the utilization of minority group members and women in criminal justice agencies. Liaison has been established with numerous other federal offices having similar responsibilities to minimize any duplication of efforts where possible. Recently, LEAA published an affirmative action manual for the agencies that are required to develop and implement equal employment opportunity programs to qualify for LEAA funding.

These are some of the achievements and accomplishments that the nation can look to with a sense of pride, but much remains to be done. Crime prevention must be a community commitment, as it is there where so many crime victims live. LEAA shares this commitment. The struggle to translate the higher aspirations and hopes of our citizens into practical results in every day life is indeed difficult. But however hard the task, it is a challenge that must be accepted—and met. Society demands no less than the best of us.

References

Bronfenbrenner, Urie. "The Origins of Alienation," *Scientific American,* August 1974, p. 53.

Jeffrey, C. Ray and Jeffrey, Ina A. "Prevention Through the Family." In W.E. Amos and C.F. Wellford (eds.), *Delinquency Prevention.* Englewood Cliffs, N.J.: Prentice-Hall, 1970.

U.S. Department of Justice, Federal Bureau of Investigation. *Crime in the United States, 1975,* Uniform Crime Reports Series. Washington, D.C.: Government Printing Office, 1976.

U.S. Department of Justice, Law Enforcement Assistance Administration. *Crime in the Nation's Five Largest Cities, Advance Report.* Washington, D.C.: Government Printing Office, 1974a.

U.S. Department of Justice, Law Enforcement Assistance Administration. *Survey of Inmates of Local Jails, Advance Report.* Washington D.C.: Government Printing Office, 1974b.

U.S. Department of Justice, Law Enforcement Assistance Administration. *Criminal Victimization in the United States, 1973, Advance Report.* Washington, D.C.: Government Printing Office, 1975a.

U.S. Department of Justice, Law Enforcement Assistance Administration, National Institute of Law Enforcement and Criminal Justice. *Design Guidelines for Creating Defensible Space.* Washington, D.C.: Government Printing Office, 1975b.

U.S. Department of Justice, Law Enforcement Assistance Administration, National Criminal Justice Information and Statistics Service. *Survey of Inmates of State Correctional Facilities, 1974, Advance Report.* Washington, D.C.: Government Printing Office, 1976.

4

Researching Black Justice: Descriptions and Implications

Samuel Barnett

As one reviews the research on the black offender, it becomes alarmingly clear that much more research is needed on black offenders in the criminal justice system. Research conducted generally has shown blacks in a negative posture and has not attempted to address the psychological struggle of the black offender. Very few studies have focused on the conflict between the prisoner's struggle to remain a dignified human being and the attempt by the prison structure to strip him of his manhood and produce the institutional cripple that most inmates become. Throughout the criminal justice system, there appears to be a lingering attempt to subjugate the black man economically, spiritually, mentally, politically, and socially, as reflected through arrest rates, jail sentences, and the operation of the prison system.

Certainly, members of other minority groups who came to America experienced discrimination and filled jails in numbers disproportionate to their representation in the total population. However, these minority groups were generally able to gain political power over their communities and to move to a position where they could control and regulate some of the flow of their people to the jails. This contrasts dramatically with the experience of blacks.

No other ethnic group has been subjected to the same experiences in America which blacks have suffered. No other group has endured as many attempts to keep them "in their place." No other group became the objects of special code words and emotional phrases ("talking back to a white man" or "was with white girls") which triggered behaviors leading to unusually long jail terms or irrational, illegal, and otherwise inexplicable actions by administrators in the criminal justice system.

The social and economic effects of the repressiveness of the criminal justice system for the black citizen has not yet been fully analyzed. Some studies which shed some light on the condition of the black citizen and the justice system are discussed below.

Police and Arrests

The police force is that part of the criminal justice system that has the most contact with the black community. Because of this continuous interaction, there are many police behaviors that should be addressed. One behavior which has been investigated has been the arrest rates of blacks. Numerous studies have been

25

conducted which highlight the unusually high number of blacks arrested and charged with violations compared to their percentage in the national population. Barnes and Teeters (1952) pointed out the discriminatory arrest procedures in the criminal justice system. Halsted (1967) likewise concluded from his research that police were more likely to arrest a black youth in discretionary situations than to arrest a white youth in similar situations. Another study (Piliavin and Briar, 1964) indicated that blacks are more likely to be questioned by the police on the street and more likely to be arrested after questioning.

Bayley and Mendelsohn (1969) studied the relationship between the Denver Police Department and Denver's black and Mexican-American communities. Their findings indicated that contacts between police and ethnic groups were determined more by ethnic group membership than by class. This conclusion does not support the viewpoint of those who assert that problems of discrimination are basically a result of class prejudice rather than racial prejudice.

In addition to the discriminatory rates of arrests, there has been a noticeably high percentage of police misconduct and brutality charges registered by black citizens. There is no doubt that the black community still harbors negative feelings about the way they have been treated by law enforcement personnel.

The addition of black policemen on predominantly white police forces is designed to eliminate some of the abuses to black communities and to enhance the image of this segment of the criminal justice system. However, in spite of the increase of blacks in police departments, racial problems still exist. Paradoxically, black applicants in many large cities of the nation have had to initiate legal means to become employed by police departments; yet, even after admission, many of them are still subject to racial friction. A report in the *New York Times* (Darnton, 1969) discussed the growing hostility between black and white police officers. Cases were cited of racial slurs written on locker room doors and fist fights between officers of different ethnic backgrounds. In some major urban cities, officers reportedly drew guns on each other. Reasons given for this racial friction were (1) the presence of a new type of black officer: younger, more assertive, and more outspoken than previous black officers; (2) an increasing number of black officers recruited from the ghetto; (3) a growing number of black officers' organizations; (4) a tendency in some departments for white officers to hold right-wing, anti-black attitudes; and (5) diverse effects of law and order campaigns as well as civil disorders by outsiders.

In other situations, some black officers are beginning to feel that they were hired as tokens to deal only with black problems and many are becoming dissatisfied with this role. This dissatisfaction has been evidenced by black officers rebelling against racial discrimination practiced by police departments. Black officers' complaints centered around discrepancies and bias in promotions, assignments, and patrols. In Omaha, Nebraska, relations between black and white officers had noticeably been affected by these discriminatory practices (Delaney, 1970). Through the combination of increased complaints of discrimination from blacks applying to police departments, and support from the black community, black police officers are growing in numbers and their organizations are receiving more support.

Based on the historical reputation of the police in the black community, many blacks believe the police function is to support and enforce the political, social, and economic interests of the dominant community and only incidentally to enforce the law. It is also suspected that whenever there is a conflict of interest between the dominant groups in this society and the less powerful groups, the police protect the interests and values of the dominant groups, usually white groups, regulating or incarcerating the less powerful, usually blacks and other minorities. Most reports and studies would tend to indicate that the behaviors of the police are certainly not inconsistent with these views.

The Courts

There have been several significant studies of the courts over the past few years. The findings from these studies precipitated many of the rulings of the Supreme Court. More favorable decisions defending the rights of the accused were rendered by Chief Justice Earl Warren during his term on the Supreme Court than at any other time in history. Without question, low income minorities were the beneficiaries of these efforts. The following three studies represent at least the substance of several other similar studies.

The first is a study conducted by Rose and Prell (1955) that was designed to test the popular assumption that the punishment given to an offender is directly related to the seriousness of the crime committed. Subjects used in this study were college students who were to act as judges in deciding punishment for offenders. They were given information describing the crime and the offenders and were then asked to select an appropriate punishment for each offender. Some very consistent trends emerged from the study. The results showed that the subjects tended to determine punishment based on the class of the defendant and the nature of the crime. Other judicial discriminatory patterns were noted from the study. Overall, subjects with upper-class backgrounds were inclined to assign longer sentences than those with lower-class backgrounds. Subjects from rural areas and small towns seemed to assign both longer prison sentences and higher fines for most crimes than subjects from large and medium sized cities. The implications of this study reflect the range of discriminatory possibilities against blacks when one considers that the overwhelming majority of judges are white, and from middle to upper socioeconomic backgrounds. In addition, the composition of a jury by social classes not representative of the accused may also increase the likelihood of a prejudicial decision.

The second study concerning the administration of the judicial system was based on data collected by the American Bar Foundation (Nagel, 1966). Using state trial court dockets for 1962, Nagel evaluated thousands of cases from 194 counties in fifty states. The study concentrated on (1) larceny, the most frequently reported crime against property, and (2) assault, the most frequently reported crime against persons. It was found that the typical safeguards of the judicial system, including preliminary hearings, bail, right to counsel, grand jury, and trial by jury, all exhibited irregularities in their application to blacks and the poor. Bail, for example, offers the accused a chance to get out of jail and prepare his case. However, about 75 percent of the indigent cases did not raise bail and stayed locked up while 79 percent of the nonindigent assault cases and 69 percent of the larceny cases did raise bail and got out. The percentage of nonindigents found guilty was consistently lower. The poor defendant was less likely to be granted probation or a suspended sentence. This applied most specifically to blacks. In larceny cases, 74 percent of guilty blacks were imprisoned in state larceny cases, against only 49 percent of guilty whites; in federal larceny cases, the percentage was 54 percent ot 40 percent respectively. These findings indicate that blacks were economic victims. They were deprived of counsel or information which would have allowed them to better prepare their cases, maintain employment, and provide for and protect their families.

Many other courtroom procedures reflected this pattern: trial by jury, delays, conviction, and sentencing all showed discriminatory behavior when the defendant was poor, black, or both. The report suggested that poverty is indeed a factor in the criminal justice system. There was little difference between northern and southern states in discrimination against black defendants. However, discriminate practices were found to be more consistent in the South at all stages from pretrial to sentencing. Nagel also concluded from the data that sentencing of the black defendant may be influenced not only by his own color, but also by the victim's color. This supports the suspicion of many in the black community that a white life is worth more than a black life. If a black kills a white he may get twenty years or death, but if a black kills another black, he may be out in five years at the most.

In a third study, Barlett and Steele (1973) made an exhaustive study of the Philadelphia courts, collecting data from 1,034 cases using over 10,000 court documents and 20,000 pages of transcripts from court proceedings to determine if there was equal justice in the court system. The analysis of the data revealed a pattern of discrimination in the court where the disposition of some cases depended solely upon who the victim was and the biases of the individual judge. The percentage of cases imprisoned was higher for blacks (64 percent) than for whites (42 percent). Blacks were more likely to receive longer jail sentences; whites were more likely to be acquitted. They concluded that there is a plural justice system: one justice for blacks and another for whites, one for persons under thirty and one for persons over thirty, one for people who commit violent crimes in a business establishment and another for people who commit violent crimes on the street.

The overwhelming opinion of most authorities is that the criminal justice system is ineffective when it comes to administering justice fairly. There are also disturbing indications that courts are unwilling to face the challenge of insuring equality. Political pressures and/or social norms continue to deliver a type of justice that results in jail time for the poor or minority defendant even when he has been fortunate enough to win his case. Further, this disruption of his family and personal life-style reinforces his belief that society accords him very little status.

In the courts there seems to be a pattern of institutional racism which serves to keep the black and poor in an unequal position before the bar of justice. Since most blacks are poor, their defenses are often handicapped by court-appointed lawyers, who are usually white, upper or middle class, and sometimes biased. These studies seem to point out clearly that American justice is not nearly so blind as it is purported to be, and in spite of the claim of equality before the law, some groups are more equal than others; blacks, the poor, and the ignorant are less equal.

Black Judges and Attorneys

As a remedy for some of the discriminatory behavior exhibited in our criminal courts, some have recommended placing more black officials in the court system. This appears to be a step in the right direction. For all but the last decade of our entire national existence, blacks have been virtually excluded from the judicial decision-making functions of our society. This same pattern has been true throughout the entire criminal justice system, including juries and law schools.

The small number of black law school graduates and the virtual nonexistence of black judges has led to a situation with white judges, white lawyers, white police officers, white complainants, and black defendants with little or no legal support. It seems that the entire machinery of law enforcement, including the court system, remains a very racially segregated and class-oriented institution in public life. In 1972, there were fewer than 300 black judges in the entire nation. Only one out of every sixty judges was black, less than 2 percent of all judges. Out of 700 federal judges, twenty were black; and out of 16,000 full-time state judges, only 258 were black (Crockett, 1972). Some see the increase in black representation in the judicial structure as an important ingredient in providing equal justice to the black community. Chrisman (1971), who believes that much of the crime in the black community is anchored in the political and economic deprivation forced on it by the dominant white political system, certainly believes this increased black participation is critical. He feels that black defendants are not judged by their peers and for a trial process to be fair, the judicial components should reflect the composition of the minority population of that community. For example, with Philadelphia having 35 percent black people in its population, 35 percent of the judges should be black. However, whether or not a quota is reached as suggested, one thing is very clear: if justice is to be truly realized, then more blacks employed in judicial capacities must become a reality.

Prisons

George Jackson, Jr., in his book, *Soledad Brother—Prison Letters of George Jackson* (1970), wrote that he had been humiliated and victimized so much in prison that he did not think he could ever recover from the experience. Malcolm X, in a similar vein, viewed his experience as a series of abusive guards and solitary confinements (Haley, 1965). The almost absolute control exercised by the prison authorities over the prisons and the prisoners has been seen even in some instances when confronted by attorneys and the courts (Hellerstein and Shapiro, 1971-1972). Prison officials have historically demonstrated that they have control over the prisoner's body; now they struggle to control the minds of the prisoners. From what Jackson and Malcolm X and others who have had a chance to evaluate prisons have said, it seems that the destruction of human dignity is primary, and rehabilitation is a minor consideration. Barnes and Teeters' (1952) research on prisons adds credibility to this position by noting that the prison experience does not rehabilitate inmates, but returns them to society in most cases much more embittered and hostile than before they entered.

The prison crisis has recently been emphasized to the public mainly by the riots and disturbances occurring in many of the prisons. To date, the only positive results that can be identified from the Attica Prison massacre is the heightened public awareness of the struggle between prison officials and prisoners.

It is clear that both judges, who as a group have articulated the need for rehabilitation, and legislative bodies, who passed the laws which have imprisoned persons, have been reluctant to exercise their power to prevent inhumane treatment in prisons. Judges and legislative bodies have been so indifferent or so politically insensitive that they have failed to intervene even when there were indications that such intervention would decrease the prisoner's likelihood of returning to jail. Only recently, on a small scale, have we begun to see some changes in this area.

It seems clear that the intolerable conditions in the prisons leading to a "revolving door" treatment process will not be resolved until society is willing to decide at least some of the significant issues. Do we want the prisons to punish or rehabilitate violators of society's norms? Are we willing to provide economic, social, and legal means to provide former inmates with a real chance for survival in our competitive society? In many cases, this means providing the released prisoner with a better start in life than he had before he violated society's norms. Is the society willing to hire, pay well, and train prison guards, parole and probation officers, and other workers who will help inmates become contributing members of a healthy society? Will legislators and other elected and responsible persons as well as the public at large commit themselves to performing a monitoring role over the way prisoners are treated in institutions?

Parole and Probation

Remediation in the prison system will undoubtedly affect the former inmate's chances on parole. There are certainly some questions that need to be raised about the practice in most states of hiring former police officers and prison guards to work as parole and probation officers. Parole and probation should be viewed as an effort to give the offender an opportunity to prove that he can make it on the outside; the supervising agency should see his role as one of providing support and encouragement. There are too many indications that the probation and parole officers perceive their role as only that of watchdog, and believe that the parolees should be returned to prison as soon as possible.

Implications for the Future

From all available indications, little change can be anticipated in the current "revolving door" treatment process of those incarcerated in jails and prisons. A significant reason for pessimism is the lack of pertinent research. Researchers continue to study mundane things as (1) prison staff manpower vs. inmate population; (2) types of hardware and its utility in supervision, managerial deployment, and efficiency of operations; and (3) bare essential needs of prisoners such as food and housing space vs. cost benefits to the taxpayer. These studies are readily funded because of their nonthreatening nature to prison authorities, but they fail to address the more basic questions underlying the whole concept of incarceration.

More research is needed in the area of humane treatment. Why is it important, for example, for an inmate to be housed in a cell, devoid of anything remotely resembling a home—a place which is cold, drab, and gray? There is evidence that certain styles of interior design can shape the mind to make it more receptive. Perhaps a beautiful eating site can convince us that we are being well fed. Why not use the same knowledge to help shape the mind of the inmate by surrounding him with a bright and cheerful environment?

In the same vein, why have institutions given prisoners numbers rather than allowing them to use their names? The detrimental effect this has on the inmate's sense of worth is not offset by the convenience of cataloging him like an animal in a box.

Another reason for pessimism is the continued refusal of American society

to accept responsibility for some of the crime committed in America. There is
an inability to understand that those who are poor or who have nothing may
resort to illegal methods to survive. It is easier to pretend that those who are
poor or in jail or both are in that condition because of some personal deficiency
rather than to believe that society needs a bottom group—the poor—in order to
function in its present structure. The findings from numerous studies have indicated that a person's interpretation of crime is influenced by race and class experiences. Crimes committed by those in high offices without punishment
provide adequate justification for crimes committed by the poor in society.
For what he feels is that he is getting his fair share. Likewise, an offender returned to society without legitimate means to get a fair share may acquire it
any way he can.

Finally, there appears to be a deliberate effort to limit the number of
qualified and "gutsy" black and other minority employees in the criminal
justice field. The premise that being black automatically means that a person
will be sensitive to and willing to operate in the best interests of minorities has
long been abandoned. There have been too many cases of blacks who remain
black only in skin pigmentation. In spite of this shortcoming, most minorities
still desire to see a greater representation of their ethnic group cruising in police
cars in their neighborhood, as lawyers defending them, as judges sitting on the
bench, and as others participating in making decisions in the criminal justice
system. Unless this is accomplished the black man still will not feel that his
needs are being met.

The need for more empirical data on the black offender is obvious. However, there is also another need that is just as pressing. All of American society
has a responsibility not only in preventing crime, but also in assuring equal
treatment in the system and insuring that inmates are returned to society with
skills to succeed rather than as broken, dependent individuals. Communities
must be willing to monitor the criminal justice system to insure that the
responsibility is being maintained. The Attica Prison riot vividly illustrates
what can happen when Americans abdicate their responsibility. It indicated
that the vast majority of Americans regarded the prison population as a poor
investment of time, money, and effort. The public did not want to take any
responsibility for the situation. The problem is that we have responsibility.
Until it is realized that the Atticas of America are everyone's responsibility,
the black man will continue to be discriminated against in the criminal justice
system.

References

Barlett, Donald and James B. Steele. "Crime and Injustice." *Philadelphia
Inquirer,* Feb. 18, 1973.

Barnes, Harry E. and Negley K. Teeters. *New Horizons in Criminology,* 2nd ed. Englewood Cliffs, N.J.: Prentice-Hall, 1952.

Bayley, David H. and Harold Mendelsohn. *Minorities and the Police.* New York: Free Press, 1969.

Chrisman, Robert. "Black Prisoners, White Law." *The Black Scholar,* April-May 1971, pp. 44-46.

Crockett, Goerge W. Jr. "Commentary: Black Judges and the Black Judicial Experience." *Wayne Law Review,* Nov. 1972, pp. 61-71.

Darnton, John. "Color Line a Key Police Problem." *New York Times,* Sept. 28, 1969, p. 1.

Delaney, Paul. "Race Friction Rising Among Policemen." *New York Times,* Sept. 13, 1970, p. 86.

Haley, Alex. *The Autobiography of Malcolm X.* New York: Grove Press, 1965.

Halsted, Donald L. *The Relationship of Selected Characteristics of Juveniles to Definitions of Delinquency.* Ed. D. Dissertation, University of Michigan, 1967.

Hellerstein, William E. and Barbara Shapiro. "Prison Crisis Litigation: Problems and Suggestions." *Buffalo Law Review* 21 (1971-1972):643-668.

Jackson, George Jr. *Soledad Brother–The Prison Letters of George Jackson.* New York: Bantam Books, 1970.

Nagel, Stuart. "The Tipped Scales of Justice." *Trans Action* (May/June 1966): 3-9.

Piliavin, Irving and Scott Briar. "Police Encounters with Juveniles." *The American Journal of Sociology* 70 (1964):206-214.

Rose, Arnold M. and Arthur E. Prell. "Does the Punishment Fit the Crime? A Study in Social Valuation." *The American Journal of Sociology* 61 (1955): 247-259.

Part II

Focus on Equality and Inequality

5

Discretionary Justice and the Black Offender

Taunya Banks

Introduction

Although formal substantive and procedural laws exist today which govern almost every aspect of the American criminal justice system, whether a person enters the system and the treatment the offender receives in the system is determined to a large degree by the exercise of informal discretionary powers by public officials at all levels. These discretionary decisions often result in the development of behaviors, attitudes and policies which are not subject to formal review through the traditional channels in the legal system.

The existence of discretionary decision-making laws has, in the main, operated to the distinct disadvantage of the minority offender. The attitudes, value system, and characteristics of the persons empowered with exercising discretion and the absence of structures or guidelines for reviewing decisions has contributed to this discretionary justice. Discretionary decisions exercised by the local patrolman in a real sense determine what laws are enforced, and against whom. Discretionary decisions made by the prosecutor determine who will be charged with an offense and what the charge will be. The judge, exercising discretionary powers with respect to sentencing, determines how long a person will remain in the system.

The use of discretion is available to criminal justice officials whenever the limits on power involve a choice among possible courses of action or inaction. With extensive latitude existing throughout the system, there is little doubt that a very great proportion of all discretionary action in the criminal justice system is either illegal or of doubtful legality. Unfortunately, discretionary decision-making is justified today because of the absence of rules to govern much discretionary justice. Davis (1969) cites two critical reasons for the absence of rules: (1) the inability of legislative bodies to fashion rules to govern all situations that must arise; and (2) the mistaken belief that the individualized justice which discretion allows produces a more equitable result.

Regardless of the justification for its existence, it is all too clear that discretionary powers in the administration of justice have been oppressive to blacks. Police procedures in the black community have been known to differ from those in the white community. Blacks, for example, are more likely to be suspected of criminal activity and be arrested. If the alleged offender is known to be black, police are more likely to make mass arrests of all blacks near the scene of the crime, something that rarely happens in the white community with

white offenders. Although release prior to indictment or trial is essential to
adequately prepare one's defense, once a black is arrested, he is not likely to
secure bail. If the offender remains in jail, he is more likely to be indicted
and convicted. Once convicted, the black or minority offender is less likely
to be placed on probation or considered for parole. All of these activities
involve some degree of informal discretionary action by officials in the
criminal justice system.

The root of the problem is deep. Janowitz (1971) describes the scope
of the problem by suggesting that the racial relationship in our country is
very much responsible for blacks being denied equal protection and due
process in criminal justice agencies. As a result, blacks generally have a more
negative attitude than whites toward police effectiveness, courtesy, conduct,
and honesty (President's Commission, 1967).

Statistical data tend to support contentions of discrepancies in the
administration of justice. Although many people inaccurately believe that all
state and federal prisons in the United States have majority inmate populations
of blacks and other minorities, there is no question that the prison population
is composed of a disproportionately high percentage of minorities. According
to the FBI 1973 Uniform Crime Reports, 26.2 percent of all arrests were of
blacks and 51.3 percent of arrests for violent crimes were of blacks (U.S.
Department of Justice, 1974).

Criminologists in general reject theories that any racial or ethnic group is
more prone to criminal activity than other groups. Some authorities believe
that crime is directly linked to economic deprivation, cultural nonassimilation,
pure prejudice, differential treatment, and social maladjustment (Barnes and
Teeters, 1959; Bontempts, 1974). This belief can be substantiated, in part, by
Janowitz's findings (1971) that race riots and other racially motivated disturbances are less likely to occur in cities where (1) there is a more racially integrated
police force; (2) there is a more representative form of local government; and
(3) there is a large percentage of blacks who are self-employed in retail trade.
All of these factors indicate a degree of economic independence as well as
cultural and social adjustments which reduce frustration in the minority community. However, since these conditions are not so prevalent in many minority
communities, the criminal justice systems must look to other devices to insure
equality of treatment in all situations.

It is, perhaps, naive to think that the mere presence of more blacks and
minorities on the police force, in the prosecutor's office, on the bench, and in
administrative positions in prisons will solve the problem of inequality in the
administration of justice. The employment of blacks in the system will likely
never be in sufficient numbers to drastically affect policy-making. In addition,
the mere presence of minorities, even in significant numbers, is often no
guarantee that discretionary powers will be exercised fairly. In fact, there has

been evidence that even some black law officers harbor negative feelings about black citizens (Reiss, 1971).

An examination of the mechanics through which discretion is exercised in four key areas in the criminal justice system will shed further light on the abuse of discretionary power.

Police

Since the beginning of the twentieth century there has been a tremendous increase in policy responsibility and activity. The increase has been caused by the rising number of criminal and regulatory offenses at every level of government. Unfortunately, there has been no equivalent increase in the size of police manpower. The discrepancy between more responsibility and limited manpower has influenced the selective enforcement of laws rather than total enforcement; it is here that the discretionary powers of the police have been increased and grossly abused. Police, and especially the individual patrolman, must exercise some discretion in determining which laws are enforced. Hence, discretion is influenced by political forces and expressed community priorities. Consequently, inconsistent policy decisions of arrest or nonarrest are often made, with differing results, from one patrolman to another in the same precinct.

Many authorities support the need for police discretion by saying that discretion is inescapable due to poor draftsmanship of criminal laws, the failure by legislative bodies to revise criminal codes to eliminate obsolete provisions, and the undesirability of highly specific criminal laws. All of these reasons are unsound. Poor draftmanship could be eliminated through aggressive court decisions voiding vague laws, which could be replaced by legislative bodies with model criminal codes. Legislative bodies could be required to revise criminal codes every five to ten years. Finally, requiring highly specific criminal laws could logically result in the enactment of laws which could be enforced and which adequately reflected community sentiment. There is no conclusive documentation that specific criminal laws are impossible or result in injustice. As law exists today, with no guidelines or principles to guide police discretion, there is neither total nor equal enforcement of the law.

Perhaps if we lived in a homogenous community the exercise of police discretion would pose no real problem. However, since ours is a heterogeneous country, police objectives in law enforcement too often fail to reflect the differences in the cultures of each community. Some limited recognition of the problem has led to increased attempts to recruit blacks and other minorities into the police force (Egerton, 1974). The problem still remains that the interests, needs, and values being enforced in most communities by most policemen are those of the dominant white culture. Law enforcement efforts seem to concentrate on protecting the white communities rather than the minority communities in which residents are more likely to be victims of crime.

There is no question that there is a need to increase police sensitivity on all levels to the interests, needs, and values of the minority community. Most recommendations for creating sensitivity have been based upon the assumption that it is impossible to eliminate or substantially minimize police discretion. Grossman (1974) suggests creative police training that takes into consideration the importance of discretionary alternatives and their applicability to a variety of situations, cultures, and subgroups.

In a report to the National Commission on the Causes and Prevention of Violence, suggestions were made for improving police sensitivity to the community (Campbell et al., 1970). While there were some excellent suggestions made for improved policy-community relations, their recommendation showed that they did not realize the danger of allowing widespread discretionary justice to be exercised at lower levels of law enforcement. For example, one recommendation for handling certain disorders suggested that the patrolman be given a wider range of *options* (discretion) such as detoxification center for drunks, family service units for handling domestic quarrels, and community service information centers to handle complaints. This recommendation only increases the opportunity for abuses of discretionary powers. The patrolman would still decide who to detain for drunkenness and who not to detain. In addition, he would also be allowed to decide who goes to jail for the offense and who is sent to a detoxification center. The existence of family service units would still not eliminate the initial discretionary decision concerning which family quarrels the police will respond to. Lastly, the community service information centers would be of doubtful aid unless they were structured to minimize discretion. As long as the employees could determine what complaints to consider or not consider the center would never engender the confidence and trust of the minority community. Procedures such as written reports stating disposition of all complaints, including reasons for not investigating some complaints, should be required. These reports should be reviewed regularly by superiors and made available to the persons who made the complaint.

It is highly probable that discretionary decisions in law enforcement can never be entirely eliminated, but they certainly can be minimized. The discretionary power that exists should only be exercised by top level police personnel. The individual patrolman should be governed strictly by administrative rules. However, corresponding action by legislative bodies directed to revising and specifying crimes and appropriating funds for increases in the size of police forces will be needed to effect change at this most crucial level of the criminal justice system.

The Prosecutor

Most citizens believe that criminal law operates almost mechanically in that the formal judicial system is constant and impervious to influences and pressures. Few realize the tremendous discretion exercised by a prosecutor in deciding to prosecute, nol prosse, or drop criminal charges against an alleged offender. Most often the prosecutor is not required by law to prosecute individuals against whom there is sufficient evidence of criminal conduct. His decision is based on his own judgment. Few jurisdictions require that any written reason be given for failure to prosecute. Even those few states which restrict the decision to prosecute generally do not limit the prosecutor's power to reduce the charge, something that frequently happens when there is plea bargaining.

A prosecutor's attitude toward an offender may be colored by many factors such as economic background, nature of the offense, public sentiment toward the case, caseload of the prosecutor's office, and the race of the offender and victim. The typical prosecutor is generally from a middle-class background and may be easily influenced by simple factors such as the dress, speech, and manners of an offender. The President's Commission on Law Enforcement and Administration of Justice (1967) notes that the prosecutor's response to his background and attitudes can result in distortions. A certain manner of dress or speech, common in another culture, may be perceived as an indication of moral unworthiness. The prosecutor may also believe that a neatly dressed, humble person is merely a victim of circumstances. In light of these considerations, it is not at all surprising to find oversentencing and undersentencing to be an everyday occurrence in our criminal justice system.

Must the discretionary power of the prosecutor be uncontrolled? Kenneth C. Davis (1969) feels that the German system of criminal justice, were the prosecutors possess no discretion with respect to prosecutions, can be a guide. In Germany the prosecutor is part of a hierarchial system headed by the minister of justice. He is directly responsible for his actions to his superiors. In addition, the German prosecutor is required to prosecute all cases where there is sufficient evidence. Those cases where the evidence is doubtful must be submitted to a judge who determines the sufficiency of the evidence and the proper interpretation of the law. The German prosecutor is not allowed to close the file on a case unless there is a written statement of the reasons. In important cases the statement must be approved by the prosecutor's superior and reported to both the victim and any suspect who has been investigated.

There can be little doubt that some of the problems that exist in the operation of the prosecutor's office are due to the fact that most prosecutors are elected, often inexperienced, and generally politically partisan. Perhaps nonpartisan elections or selection of prosecutors on the basis of merit would reduce abuses of discretion, but the human element would still be a factor which could result in further discriminatory practices. Removal of discretion is still the best solution for assuring equal treatment.

The American Jury System

Kalvin and Zeisel (1966), in a major study conducted during the 1950s on the American jury system, found that racial prejudice influenced jury decisions. Smith and Pollack (1972) inferred that poor and black people are vastly under-represented in all juries throughout the United States. Nevertheless, the courts have been very reluctant to interfere with jury selection practices in this country. In the landmark case *Swain* v. *Alabama* (1965), the United States Supreme Court held that blacks could be tried by juries on which there were no members of their race. As long as the method used for selecting juries was not a conscious or deliberate attempt to exclude blacks or minorities from juries, no constitutional rights have been violated. However, the court has refused to seriously consider other practices which allow racial imbalances in the composition of juries.

One of the common legal procedures that can be used prejudicially is the preemptory challenges to remove prospective black jurors from the panel. No reason for the exclusion need be given. Some might argue that the numerical limit on these challenges is a sufficient check on potential abuse. However, this argument is valid only in those jurisdictions with a substantial number of black citizens who are subject to call for jury duty.

A large number of jurisdictions have used voter registration rolls as a means of selecting prospective jurors. Unfortunately, blacks, other minorities, and the poor are not registered in as great numbers as whites and middle and upper income groups. The result is that poor and minority offenders are tried by juries which do not adequately reflect their cultural and economic background. These juries may have little understanding of the offender's life-style or environmental influences and may be hostile toward the offender because of his background.

Since little can be done about jury discretion short of abolishing jury trials, a possible solution to abuses of discretionary powers by juries lies in restructuring the jury system. Derrick Bell (1973) has suggested several methods which might produce significant numbers of blacks and minorities on juries trying cases directly affecting the interest of minority litigants or the minority community. He suggested redrawing jury districts in the northern urban areas so that each minority community would constitute a jury district and require that every jury be proportionately representative of the black population in the heavily black areas of the rural South. In addition, it should be required that the jury be selected in civil cases from the community where the action arose, and in criminal cases where the crime occurred.

It will continue to be difficult for minority offenders to believe that they are receiving equal justice before juries as long as they are judged solely by juries comprised of persons from different cultural and economic backgrounds. There may be some merit to that belief. It would be hard for an all white southern jury to comprehend the contention of a young black political radical that he shot a policeman in self-defense because he believed that his life was endangered because he was black. Although they may end up with the same verdict, there is a chance that a jury composed of some ethnic jurors could evaluate the evidence without being prejudiced by the color of the defendant or his political or cultural beliefs. This would truly be justice.

Judicial Sentencing

Judges in the American legal system have almost unchecked powers to fashion sentences. For example, some offenses are punishable by a fine, imprisonment, or both; the judge has three options. If the judge chooses imprisonment, he has the additional option of placing the offender on probation, giving him a "split-sentence" (part imprisonment, part probation), or sentencing the offender to the full term. Even in the last situation the judge has tremendous discretion in determining the length of the sentence. Criminal statutes only compound the problem. The federal kidnapping law, for example, authorizes sentences for any number of years or for life. This is not at all uncommon, even on the federal level. Not only are extremely high maximum sentences a problem, but an even more common flaw is mandatory minimum sentences. This means that the convicted offender often has no way of predicting with reliability whether he will be released on probation, be given a short term, or be sentenced for a long period of time. This problem is further compounded by the fact that the United States Supreme Court has held that it will not review a sentence based only on the assertion that it was too harsh (*Townsend* v. *Burke*, 1948).

Once again, the human factor is a great influence on the length of sentences and can include such things as geographic background and political or religious beliefs. Traditionally, judges imposing sentences have considered the gravity of the offense, the existence of a prior criminal record, and the offender's age and background. Nevertheless, there are no set guidelines to determine the relevant criteria to be used and their relative importance. The criteria and importance assigned them depend in large part upon the individual beliefs and bias of each judge.

A 1958 federal statute authorizes the establishment of sentencing institutes and joint councils on sentencing which are designed to formulate criteria, policies, and standards for sentencing. The statute is an excellent piece of legislation, but few jurisdictions have chosen to make widespread use of it. Other attempts to provide solutions to the problem of sentencing disparities include the Model Sentencing Act and Model Penal Code of the American Law Institute (U.S.

Department of Justice, 1975). Both of these codes recommend limiting judicial discretion. They recommend increased use of probation and fewer severe sentences. Presentencing investigations are mandatory in certain cases and the offender has some opportunity to challenge investigative reports. Severe sentences are to be supported by findings of specified facts which are to be incorporated in the record. Both codes establish major new categories such as "dangerous offenders," "atrocious crime" (Model Act), "persistent offender," "professional criminal," "a dangerous mentally abnormal," and "a multiple offender" (Penal Code). Each of these terms are elaborately defined in order to guide judicial discretion.

Widespread discretionary powers for judges may allow "individualized" justice, but "individualized" justice does not necessarily mean equal justice. Until better standards are established, blacks and other minorities will continue to be underpenalized for certain types of offenses involving black crimes and overpenalized for other offenses including robbery and black on white rape (Overby, 1972; Bell, 1973). Where there is any discretion, no matter how limited, abuses will probably occur. Until the courts are willing to provide appellate review of sentencing, disparity will continue to occur and will most adversely affect the minority offender.

Conclusion

In order to insure impartiality of treatment regardless of race or economic status, standards and guidelines must be established concerning the exercise of discretionary power. The recommendations proposed for controlled discretion in the administration of justice require legislative action. Because legislators are reluctant to intervene, it is doubtful that any substantive change will eliminate all the abuses of discretion in the near future. The only other course of action lies in administrative action by the police departments, the prosecutors' offices, and the courts. The process may be slow and not as effective as legislative action. Administrative rules enacted by each of these units would attempt to establish specific structures and guidelines for the performance of their discretionary functions. Unfortunately, the police, prosecutors, and the courts are all overloaded, understaffed, and financially strained. As long as these factors persist, these units will continue to resist recommended reforms in their areas.

The future for the black offender looks very bleak because change must occur in all of these areas before impartiality can be achieved. Without change, there is little hope of drastically reducing the crime rate among blacks in this country. As long as discretion is used to the disadvantage of a group because of race, culture, or economic level, blacks will continue to be discriminated against in the criminal justice system. It is highly unlikely that the attitude of the majority race in this country toward blacks will change sufficiently to cause them to be truly concerned with black crime and the black offender. It is much easier to remove from the larger society those persons who have outlived their usefulness than to seek the means to insure their meaningful participation in such a society. What is needed is a restructuring of society. Reform measures are merely bandages, only covering the problems but never really solving them.

References

Barnes, Harry E. and Negley K. Teeters. *New Horizons in Criminology,* 3rd ed. Englewood Cliffs, N.J.: Prentice-Hall, 1959.

Bell, Derrick A. Jr. *Race, Racism and American Law.* Boston: Little Brown, 1973.

Bontempts, Alex. "Black Crime: a Special Report." *Race Relations Reporter,* Nov. 1974, pp. 12-15.

Campbell, James S.; Joseph R. Sahiel; and David P. Stang. *Law and Order Reconsidered: Report of the Task Force on Law and Law Enforcement to the National Commission on the Causes and Prevention of Violence.* New York: Praeger, 1970.

Davis, Kenneth C. *Discretionary Justice: A Preliminary Inquiry.* Baton Rouge, La.: Louisiana State University Press, 1969.

Egerton, John. "Minority Police: How Many are There?" *Race Relations Reporter,* Nov. 1974, pp. 19-21.

Grossman, Brian. "The Discretionary Enforcement of Law." In Sawyer F. Sylvester, Jr. and Edward Sagarin (eds.), *Politics and Crime,* New York: Praeger, 1974, pp. 65-75.

Janowitz, Morris. "Patterns of Collective Racial Violence." In Leon Radzinowitz and Marvin E. Wolfgang (eds.), *Crime and Justice, Vol. 2. The Criminal In The Arms of The Law.* New York: Basic Books, 1971.

Kalvin, Harry Jr. and Hans Zeisel. *The American Jury.* Chicago: University of Chicago Press, 1966.

Overby, Andrew. "Discrimination in the Administration of Justice." In Charles E. Reasons and Jack Keykendall (eds.), *Race, Crime and Justice.* Pacific Palisades, Calif.: Goodyear Publishing Co., 1972, pp. 264-276.

President's Commission on Law Enforcement and Administration of Justice. *The Challenge of Crime in a Free Society.* Washington, D.C.: Government Printing Office, 1967.

Radzinowitz, Leon and Marvin E. Wolfgang. "Public Attitudes Toward the Police." In Leon Radzinowitz and Marvin E. Wolfgang (eds.), *Crime and Justice, vol. 2. The Criminal In the Arms of the Law.* New York: Basic Books, 1971.

Reiss, Albert J. Jr. *The Police and the Public.* New Haven, Conn.: Yale University Press, 1971.

Schrag, Clarence. *Crime and Justice: American Style.* Rockville, Md.: National Institute of Mental Health, Center for Studies of Crime and Delinquency, 1971.

Smith, Alexander B. and Harriet Pollack. *Crime and Justice in a Mass Society.* New York: Holt, Rinehart and Winston, 1972.

Swain v. Alabama, 380 U.S. 202, 1965.

Townsend v. Burke, 334 U.S. 736, 741, 1948.

U.S. Department of Justice, Federal Bureau of Investigation. *Crime in the United State, 1973, Uniform Crime Reports.* Washington, D.C.: Government Printing Office, 1974.

U.S. Department of Justice, Law Enforcement Assistance Administration. *Compendium of Model Correctional Legislation and Standards,* 2nd ed. American Bar Association Commission on Correctional Facilities and Services and Council of State Governments, June 1975.

Challenge for the Judicial System: Economic and Racial Equality

George W. Crockett, Jr.

The problems that blacks face in the criminal justice system today, as employees, officers, and clients all relate to race and color discrimination. This is true whether one considers appointments and elections, promotions and layoffs, illegal arrest and police brutality, exorbitant bail and preventive detention, overcharging and plea bargaining, the high cost and/or inefficiency of defense counsel, the disparity in sentencing, and the inability of correctional institutions to rehabilitate and thereby reduce recidivism. All of these deficiencies have racial connotations.

However, it is a grave mistake to assume that race and/or color is the only issue, or even the primary issue. The fact is, even if blacks were accorded equal treatment in the system, the problems they face would remain unsolved and the system would not be any more tolerable. This is so because the evils which inhere in our criminal justice system are neither race nor color oriented; they are class oriented. They would continue to exist even if race and color distinctions were eliminated, because blacks and other non-white groups in this country are poor, propertyless, and economically powerless. The basic problem faced in improving the criminal justice system is ending the discrimination against the poor—regardless of race, creed, or color. This is the prime lesson that every perceptive black and every friend of blacks should have learned during the past ten years.

Today most, if not all, of the more facile forms of race and color discrimination are on the way out or have disappeared. Blacks are no longer turned back or openly Jim-Crowed at public places, and more and more blacks are gaining influential positions in both industry and government. However, the basic discrimination resulting from group as well as individual poverty is still present. The University of Alabama is open, but only to those who can afford it. The number of black law enforcement officers, correction and probation officers, attorneys, judges, and court attaches has increased manifold, but so has the number of black and non-white youths who are caught up in the criminal justice system because of their poverty.

The reasoning, then, that leads one to think race or color is the dominant factor affecting blacks in the criminal justice system and subsequently that its elimination is the solution, is analogous to believing that the evils of inferior public schools for blacks can be corrected by insisting that black and white children alike must attend the same inferior schools; or believing that the present layoffs and other employment hardships encountered by blacks as a result of union seniority rules can be overcome by abolishing these rules and discharging blacks and whites simultaneously and in equal numbers.

Just as equal access to *inferior* schools or equal *unemployment* will not better the condition of blacks, a single-minded struggle, centered around improving the criminal justice system for blacks only will not better the condition. The poor of whatever race, creed, color, or ethnic origin are all natural allies in the struggles for justice. They share the same hardships. We must seek them out and work with them. We must not alienate them. Until the evils of the present system are eliminated for all, they will not be eliminated for any.

The American criminal justice system as orchestrated in the Bill of Rights and the Civil War amendments was intended to be classless, with special emphasis on protecting the weak and propertyless from the excesses of the rich and powerful. But in practice the system has become just the opposite. The emphasis of the criminal justice system today is on property and the protection of property, on wealth and the protection of wealth, on power and the preservation of power.

The famous lawyer Clarence Darrow once remarked that he never saw a rich man in prison. That is as accurate today as it was seventy-five years ago. The criminal court dockets are overburdened and jails are inhumanly crowded and mismanaged. However, those accused who can afford to have carefully-selected attorneys work intensively on their behalf are less likely to go to jail than are poor people who commit crimes. Despite the enormity of white collar crime, as compared with the run-of-the-mill criminal courtroom parade of petty thefts and breaking and entries, the sentences meted out to rich felons are remarkably light. Look, for example, at the Watergate criminals or the Vice President Agnew affair. For felonies which have rocked the nation and violated the most sacred rights, these criminals are receiving lesser sentences than many shoplifters or car thieves brought before the city courts.

Economic crises—such as America is now experiencing—are inherent characteristics of a decaying capitalist system. History shows that social and economic stress lead to attacks on civil liberties. It is reflected today in the studied attempt by the Burger Supreme Court to restrict or nullify many of the precedential rulings of the Warren Supreme Court in the area of criminal procedure—rulings which made the procedural guarantees of the federal Bill of Rights binding upon state courts and state officials.

The new targets of the anti-civil libertarians will be many, and many will be vulnerable. They will not necessarily be blacks, although blacks will continue to suffer in disproportionate numbers. They will not necessarily be workers, although the unorganized are still incapable of protecting themselves. The liberals and radicals will always be fair game because they will always pose a threat to the established order. Nevertheless, armed with constitutional defenses, they have won hard-fought battles in the courts, on picket lines, and in freedom marches. They have dared to test the Constitution and to make the Constitution work.

Today it is the poor who are defenseless. It is the poor, trapped in ghettos, who are fast becoming majorities in the large cities. It is the poor who have been forgotten in long neglected and super-depressed areas like Appalachia, the rural South and Southwest, and even in Michigan's upper peninsula. It is the poor who have steadily lost important ground in relation to all other economic groups.

The poor today are the largest and most oppressed minority. It is not sufficient to assume that welfare, emergency jobs, or other Band-Aid remedies will protect them. They need jobs—permanent jobs—if they are to avoid being grist for the criminal justice mill. They need genuine educational opportunities. These are not obtained by busing students to strange schools in hostile neighbor-hoods, but can come only with the proper expenditure of money and other resources to eliminate all substandard education. The poor need decent housing, food, health safeguards, and a fighting chance to begin to climb out of the bottomless pit of their ghetto existence. Until these basic needs are fulfilled, they will be unable to defend themselves against the slings and arrows of a hostile and selfish society which continues to deny them the liberty of a decent life. Until they acquire a decent existence, the greatest of all liberties, they will not only remain defenseless in the battle to maintain their other liberties, but they will also continue to fill the criminal court dockets and our prisons.

Blacks have gained a foothold and climbed part way up the ladder of social equality, but the ascent to economic equality is being effectively blocked. Blacks have come a long way since 1954, but still have a long way to go before the war for economic justice is won. The challenge for the here and now is to continue the struggle at a higher level, on a wider plane, and with a deeper understanding. The challenge is to reach out and grasp the hands of all others who suffer from an economic system that inevitably makes them the victims of a chronically unjust criminal justice system. The challenge is to work cease-lessly to eliminate every vestige of economic classism from the criminal justice system.

The judicial system, of the three great divisions of government, has been most helpful to blacks. In the past, it has been a refuge from the discriminatory actions of the other two branches. Judges stand at the apex of the criminal justice system and the system succeeds or fails in the quest for justice depending upon what this segment does or fails to do. It is appropriate, therefore, that the public concern itself with the role that judges, particularly the black judges, perform in improving the system and advocating rights for the poor, the power-less, and the oppressed.

The court system is often described as an objective mirror of changes in our country. In truth, the courts have played a much more active and aggressive role. Unfortunately, our judiciary has aided and abetted nearly every crusade which carried the approbation and expressed the needs of the prevailing dominant economic forces in our society. The courts have not only been arbiters, they have been protectors of the American power wielders. The historical commitment of our courts has been to maintain the rights and privileges of a few as more important than either the spirit or the letter of the law would suggest. No other interpretation satisfactorily explains, for example, the extermination policy toward the American Indians or the continuing subjection of black Americans, even after adoption of the Thirteenth, Fourteenth, and Fifteenth Amendments.

The much vaunted "independence" claimed by the judiciary is, of course, a myth. No apparatus of the state is independent. The judge relies on the city, county, state, or federal government for his position and for the advantages of his office. He is subservient to higher courts and to their approval of his conduct and his rulings. He is accountable to associations of his peers, lawyers, judges, and prosecutors, for his reputation. He is responsible to the executive and legislative branches of government, which have the power to erode, replace, or nullify the effect of his rulings.

Despite these limitations, a judge dedicated to change and to progress can find considerable latitude within the existing system. This arena of power, circumscribed though it its, affords surprising opportunities for judicial and, ultimately, legal change. After two hundred years of experience with the constitution, new change agents are appearing to alter substantially the character, the selection, and the response of considerable sections of the American judiciary.

When changes occur, they impinge first on those areas of the court facing greatest tension and pressure. One such area in the last decade has been the urban court system. The massive postwar migration of southern rural blacks to the cities and the equally sizable exodus of middle class whites to the suburbs have profoundly altered the composition of major urban centers. New York and Chicago, the two largest cities, have seen their population change in three decades from 10 percent to 25-35 percent black. In Detroit, traditionally a favorite target area for Alabama blacks migrating north, the rate has gone from 14 percent in 1940 to more than 50 percent today.

The changes generated by the growing numerical and political importance of blacks have now begun to affect substantially the most sensitive and deep-rooted elements of our society. One of these is the composition of the judiciary. In 1950, there were not more than twenty black judges in the entire United States—federal, state, and local. As of April 1974 there were more than 332 black judges in thirty-six states, the federal government, and the Virgin Islands. In the recorder's courts of Detroit, nine of the twenty-three judges were black. Nearly half of the court personnel were non-white. The police department, although lagging in integration, was almost 20 percent black. This rapid change in the complexion of our courts constitutes a clear and direct assault on the largest and most obstinate obstacle to democracy in our country: its historical refusal to follow the spirit and the letter of our laws, especially with regard to racism.

The history of the United States has left its indelible imprint on the minds and souls of its black citizens. Such lofty and inspiring national concepts as liberty, equality, and justice have had different meanings for different people. To blacks, in all areas, the vibrations generated by those noble principles are hemmed in by experience itself, by a history of discrimination, segregation, and second-class citizenship. It is not surprising, therefore, that a black judge would be more sensitive to some of the subleties of the law and the Constitution, especially as they describe and define the rights of the individual. It is not surprising, as a consequence, that black judges, especially in our criminal courts, have begun to play the role of the conscience for the entire judiciary. The arrival of black judges at our tribunals has already begun to produce dramatic changes not only in the processing of cases, the treatment of the accused, and the conduct of hearings and trials, but also in the interpretation of the law itself.

Reflect for a moment on the traditional pattern of treatment of a black apprehended for a suspected criminal act. He is arrested by a white policeman and taken to a white desk sargeant or jailer, often forcibly and violently. He is arraigned before a white magistrate, whose clerk, stenographer, and other assistants are white. If there is a trial, he retains or is assigned a white lawyer, and the prosecution, the judge, the jury, and just about everyone symbolizing the force and authority of the law is white. To blacks, the very face of the law has been a white face. The apparatus, the people, and even the atmosphere setting the stage upon which a black has pled for justice have been devoid of even the *appearance* of justice.

The presence of blacks in the courtroom has led to momentous progress in our entire system of justice. The impact of that change is felt not only by the accused, but by the legal structure itself. Black participation in the legal framework has moved the balance of power in many spheres. In Detroit, for example, a series of inquiries and judicial motions led to the discovery that the criminal court administration had been following a deliberate, consistent policy of excluding from jury panels a wide variety of people who did not fit the middle class mold. Young people, "hippies," blacks, and others judged undesirable by officials were never selected for jury duty. This situation was eventually exposed and corrected.

Another example of courtroom changes generated by the new influence of blacks concerns the bail system. The concept of bail as a security guarantee rather than as a tool of punishment and discrimination has been opened for reexamination in many cities. The manner in which confessions may legally be obtained is also being redefined. The adequacy of legal representation for poor litigants is being reviewed. The time lapse between apprehension and trial is being tested in the courts. The frequently inadequate or legally-tainted evidence presented by the prosecutor and the police is being challenged openly, not only by Legal Aid defense attorneys, but even by the judges.

Each of these legal phenomena is old to the law but still new to too many of our courts and judges. Each has moved the application of the law toward a greater conformity with the letter of the law. Each has forced a stricter observance of constitutional liberties, which were always promised and too rarely granted.

It would be an oversimplification to ascribe these changes solely to the presence of blacks on the bench. However, it is necessary to emphasize the unique role of blacks as catalytic agents reinforcing and accelerating the pace of the American march toward legal justice.

The American society, the saying goes, is one of laws, not of men. It is for the protection of the many that this must be so, but in this society the law must be subservient to the people. It is within the people's power to retain, to alter, or to eliminate those laws which do not properly serve their needs. Now, in these last two decades, the people have moved farther and faster than ever before to insist upon the exercise of their power. The results are only beginning to take hold, and they bode well for the strength and resilience of our democracy.

7

Elitism: Perpetuation Through Incarceration

Laurence French

The awareness of the existence of judicial discrimination in America is by no means new information, for much has been written on the concept of dualistic justice and selective discretion along race, sex, and class lines. However, merely acknowledging the existence of this social process says little about the nature and extent of the problem. In reality, the use of judicial discrimination, as reflected by incarceration statistics, has been a viable vehicle for imposing and maintaining superordinate controls upon society, especially in the historically white, male-dominated South.

The boundary-maintenance perspective of relative justice is crucial to the position that judicial discrimination is used in our society to maintain the status quo. This orientation, based upon the works of Durkheim, Erikson, and others, assumes that justice is a culturally relativistic concept whose flexibility is determined by the control boundaries that define the extent of desirable and undesirable social behavior. Also central to the function of relative justice is Pareto's (1968) view of social control and power based on class superiority and movement among classes (circulation of elites). The boundary-maintenance orientation, coupled with Pareto's relativistic concept of social control and power, provides the basis for a considerably different image of justice than that posited by the ideal criminal justice mandate where "justice" is often viewed as an absolute variable rather than a socially and politically defined control variable.

Discriminatory Justice

Much of the literature on discriminatory justice lends support, either directly or indirectly, to the boundary-maintenance superordinate-subordinate control theme. Jack Douglas (1970) spoke on the broad application of dualistic justice in our society, noting that it permeated society's primary and secondary relationships. Some investigators, such as Clark (1965) and Kvaraceus and Miller (1976) wrote on the effects that institutions, especially the educational system, have in perpetuating classist, sexist, and racist standards in our society.

Other investigators have addressed their research to the more particular issue of discriminatory justice. Some have suggested that poverty breeds crime at the hand of the criminal justice apparatus since the existing criminal justice ideals apparently do not apply to the lower class members of society. This lower class status results in the poor being arrested more often, convicted more frequently, and sentenced more harshly.

Wolfgang (1958), in a study comparing commuted death sentences between whites and blacks, found that a more significant proportion of blacks than whites were executed and concluded that blacks do not receive equal consideration for commutation of the death penalty. More recently, the McKay Report (1972), on the Attica uprising, documented racist policies at the New York state prison facility that played a major role in the subsequent riot and deaths. Discriminating practices included less pay, fewer desirable jobs, and general harassment of the black and Puerto Rican inmates.

Garfinkel's (1949) work focused more specifically on judicial racist discrimination in the South. In an eleven-year study of the North Carolina judiciary, he found a distinctive bias regarding the adjudication of interracial homicides. Blacks killing whites were considered "sacred" matters with stress placed on getting the "nigger" responsible. Some white versus white homicide cases also were considered sacred depending on the social class of the victim in relation to that of the offender. However, blacks killing blacks and whites murdering blacks were considered "secular" issues with little sentiment involved. Along similar lines, Overby (1972), in a review of the administration of justice in the South, noted that many tactics were employed which deliberately denied blacks equal justice. These include inaccessibility to fair defense counsel, prejudicial prosecution, biased judges and juries, and discriminatory bail practices.

Political Aspects of Justice

Becker (1963) adds meaning to the above discussion of selective and discriminatory justice by analyzing the political factors involved in these processes. He suggested that it is those who possess political and economic power in society who are responsible for defining and instituting relative morality. More explicitly, he inferred that social groups create deviance by arbitrarily defining certain behaviors as deviant. This process of legislating ethical behavioral standards leads to the development of new control and enforcing agencies which, in turn, are instrumental in either creating new classes of outsiders or reinforcing the stigma of existing marginal groups. It seems that these control groups' function is not so much to control the outsiders as much as it is to publicize and draw attention to their negative image.

Erikson (1966) asserts that the process of labeling and publicizing marginal groups by the societal control agencies is a natural process in that it occurs in all societies at all times. The label of deviance defines for the rest of the society the normative limits of the flexible social boundaries at any given time. This labeling of deviance explains, in part, why many social institutions whose manifest purpose is to discourage deviant behavior actually operate in such a manner

as to reinforce and perpetuate behavior labeled as deviant. Labeling itself can
become a self-fulfilling prophecy. Examples of this self-fulfilling prophecy are
the correctional institutions which gather marginal people labeled deviants into
tightly segregated groups, and provide them an opportunity to teach each other
the skills and attitudes of a deviant career. Often these institutions encourage
and provoke their wards to use deviant skills by reinforcing their sense of alienation from the rest of society.

Quinney (1969) likewise focused on the politicality of the judicial process
questioning the assertion that justice was rationally and fairly determined and
administered at the hands of the criminal justice apparatus. Quinney contends
that it is not general social interest but rather special political interest which
determine the nature of laws. He sees law as consisting of specialized rules
which are created and interpreted in a politically organized society based on an
interest group structure with an unequal distribution of power.

The Elite Group

Coser (1956), in his work on the functions of conflict, provided additional insight to the maintenance of the elite group concept through his statement that
out-group hostilities increase in-group cohesion. Goode (1967) and Gusfield
(1963) related this process to the American power elite and its justifications of
the American ideals supported by the Protestant Ethic and Social Darwinism.
Goode (1967) supported the position that there are numerous negative functions
or dysfunctions created through the process of institutionalized social inequality
or stratification. He noted that many in-group mechanisms exist which protect
inept members of the elite group. Strong informal support for patterns of
"insulation" are used to insure both in-group occupation of a strata as well as
the prevention of out-group encroachment which may result if universal competition was in fact the norm. Gusfield (1963) applied the concepts of political
power elitism and class polarization in his work on the temperance movement
where he viewed this phenomenon as a symbolic crusade with far-reaching
social and moral significance. Here moral issues are seen as attempts by elitist
interest groups to gain dominance, recognition, and prestige of their life-style
within the total society. The political nature of such moral controversies are
crucial since legal, political recognition of one group's ideals symbolizes respectability and prestige for the elitist group while at the same time defining
the social distance between that group and others in the society.

Once the elitist group has established its moral imperatives and imposed
them upon the rest of society in the form of laws, these are then interpreted
in terms of the American ideals. That is, the concepts of equality and free
competition for scarce positions of power, prestige, and wealth is superimposed
on these ideals. This has given the false impression that these ideals provided

the basis for formation of the elite strata and that their moral and legal ideals actually benefit the entire society.

The contradictions between the American ideals of open and free competition and those of elitist self-interest are quite varied, resulting in a general misunderstanding of how and why polar class differences and double standards of justice exist in our society. Scheler (1961), the cultural phenomenologist, however, questioned the merits and logic of imposing a single, idealistic value system upon a heterogeneous society. He elaborated on Hume's idea of cultural relativistic social mechanisms of control. Basic to his argument is the many subcultural variations that are ignored by the unicultural, dominant value system that makes the system partisan rather than universal. In his theory of social structure and anomie, Merton (1966) presented a similar argument noting that because of society's unicultural, dominant value system, many members of society are denied access to legitimate means of desirable ends and must adapt to alternative cultural life-styles or resort to deviant modes of achieving the coveted societal success goals. Coping mechanisms include innovation, ritualism, retreatism, and rebellion. Dahrendorf (1968) provided the pragmatic, philosophical argument supportive of this school of thought. He argued that positing self-interest as the motivating factor for human and group behavior probably came closer to explaining social reality than does the "rationalist" who argues that man's motivation is governed by altruism and innate rationality and that society pursues harmonious and equitable order.

Social Dichotomies

One aspect of the political interest phenomenon is the maintenance of social dichotomies. In our society, these are based on sex, class, and race. While the categorization process, for the most part, is an artifical one based on elitist self-interest, intricate social defense mechanisms have emerged attempting to explain it in terms of the American dream. Out-group members (according to their sex, class, and race) suffer a common fate: exclusion from the social, political, and economic power structure.

Discrimination against females (especially white females) differs somewhat from that directed toward the lower class males and minority members. Discrimination has been somewhat political, but most noticeably it is an economic exclusion in terms of being deprived of access to the top level employment opportunities. The female has basically been assigned "positive" roles as the primary socializing agent and preserver of family morality. Due to the females favorable, yet submissive, position within society, the male social leaders have developed an elaborate network of secondary controls designed to protect the "susceptible" female. This protective element, while prevalent nationwide, has historically been most evident in the South, especially among the white dominant class.

The class factor overlaps both the sex and race categories, while at the same time including a substantial number of white males, making it the most inclusive category. In many northern urban areas, the poor and minority members are one and the same. In the South, where the population distribution is still largely rural, there are many poor whites coexisting with poor blacks. While both the poor whites and blacks are politically, socially, and economically powerless, the black's lot has historically been worse; blacks were often the scapegoats for the frustrated lower class whites. While they may be powerless, poor whites have generally been more socially acceptable to the majority population than poor blacks.

Justification of these social dichotomies, especially those related to class and race, are rationalized in terms of the American Dream by both the Protestant Ethic and Social Darwinism. So as not to question the American ideals of universal equality and accessibility to coveted, prestige positions within our society, the existing social stratas were attributed to innate moral and/or biological inferiority rather than to any social structural inequalities.

The Criminal Justice System

It follows that those possessing social, political, and economic power also manipulate the societal control mechanisms: education, economic, political, and legalistic institutions. The ruling power elite establishes what Goode (1969) terms "epistemological methodology," a specific design for imposing and implementing the governing body's values upon the rest of society. The criminal justice apparatus best represents the end result of the selective control processes. It is a unique control mechanism in that its mandate allows it to legally punish societal members adjudged deviant. It can select in and select out various offenders.

Sykes (1967) and others have suggested that there is a noticeable attribution process of offenders at every stage in criminal justice; the President's Task Force Report documented it. Sykes (1967) pointed out that crimes are "lost" at every stage in the criminal justice process with a precipitous drop in the number of cases as the system moves from the commission of a crime to the application of penal sanctions. The President's Task Force Report (President's Commission, 1967) showed the extent of selection using the 1965 FBI crime index. For the seven index crimes (homicide, forcible rape, aggravated assault, robbery, burglary, grand larceny, and auto theft) 1,780,000 offenses were reported; 727,000 were cleared by arrest; 177,000 persons were charged; 160,000 were sentenced; and only 63,000 were incarcerated.

Quinney (1970) argued that these statistics only tell part of the story because criminal statistics, regardless of their accuracy, do not indicate the true nature of criminality in that they do not account for unreported offenses. He feels that unreported offenses or "hidden criminality" probably accounts for the majority of crimes committed in our society. Current research on crime in

municipalities strongly supports this premise by showing that reported crimes
represent less than half of those actually committed. Quinney suggested that all
human behavior has a probability of becoming defined as criminal; however,
only a portion of all cases are officially processed and labeled as criminal in one
or more of the adjudication stages.

Kaplan (1973), offering an explanation as to why this selection occurs, con-
tended that a subtle process occurs in the criminal justice system whereby ideal
practices are modified through the use of informal, administrative techniques
involving biased individual judgments and discretion rather than judicial rules
and procedures. This explanation, together with Quinney's political self-interest
concept, presents a contorted picture of justice, one quite removed from that
portrayed by criminal justice ideals.

The criminal justice components, law enforcement, the judiciary, and corrections, each in its own way has been licensed by society to punish, even exe-
cute, deviant members of society. Law enforcement agencies are the only
civilian forces allowed to bear and use arms in enforcing the law, the judiciary
has the power to sentence, and corrections enforces judicial sentences. Most
importantly, this powerful control apparatus is under the direction of the power
elite, the encumbent political structure.

Analysis of a Power Elite System

Political manipulation of control agencies occurs throughout the country, but
has been more visible and evident in the South where the power structure has
changed little over the last century. Because the power elite has been stable, it
has been able to be more blatant and open about its overall societal control
design, one that often incorporates institutionalized racial discrimination. The
consistency and stability of the power elite can be reflected in the operation
of the institutions which the power structure controls. The following investigation analyzes one such system, that of North Carolina.

The Setting

Our society is a violent one as many scholars have attested (Palmer, 1972,
Skolnick, 1969). One element of the National Commission of the Causes and
Prevention of Violence dealt with the history of violence in America (Graham
and Gurr, 1970). They noted that violence has long been one of the characteristics most frequently attributed to Southerners with their history of duels,
slavery, lynching, chain gangs, and brutal police tactics. The FBI's Uniform
Crime Reports bear this out, showing the South as consistently having the
highest murder rate in the country. Violence, then, seems to be the general
norm concerning not only southern behavioral patterns in general, but involves
also the response patterns of the formal control agencies as well.

North Carolina historically has fit this image well. Famous for its part in the 1838 Cherokee removal, better known as the "Trail of Tears," the state is also well known for its active role in the Civil War. Other interesting examples of control violence include the long tenure of the chain gang and the decades of lynch mob rule following the war between the states.

Steiner and Brown (1927), in their book *The North Carolina Chain Gang,* notice that prior to the Civil War there was no state prison and all punishment was dispensed at the county or local level. Jails were used only as temporary holding facilities. Following the Civil War, however, the chain gang was developed. Prisoners were placed in enclosed, barred wagons, which could be transported from job to job. Shackles and chains as well as the ship and sweatbox were the normal and legal methods of control. These controls were enforced by county officials who originally regulated the North Carolina chain gang system which involved mostly misdemeanors since felons were handled by the state.

Barnes and Teeters (1959) referred to the Southern chain gang as "the American Siberia," stating that they were not only discriminatory but manifested some of the cruelest punishment and inhumane treatment ever recorded in American penal history. Blacks made up the vast majority of offenders who were sentenced to the chain gang in North Carolina. According to 1874 North Carolina records, 455 prisoners were in the state prison: 384 were black and 71 were white. In 1875 there were 647 prisoners, of whom 569 were black and 78 were white, while in 1878, 846 were black, 105 were white, and one was American Indian. On the average, the county chain gang ratio was four to one black.

A parallel development, again concerning county penal practice, was the lynching era in the South. According to Ginzburg's (1962) work, *100 Years of Lynching,* most lynching of blacks in North Carolina occurred during the late 1890s and ended in 1910. By coincidence, lynching subsided when the state absorbed all capital punishment into its jurisdiction in 1910.

The uniqueness of the North Carolina criminal justice system does not rest solely with its correctional system. Still on the law books, although unenforcible, is Statute GS 14-181, miscegenation, a felony. In addition, judges can declare escaped convicts "outlaws," which in effect allows any citizen to pursue these persons and present them to the court dead or alive. In April 1974, two felons who had escaped from a minimum security camp were declared as such.

Another current North Carolina criminal justice system controversy concerns the state's attempt to reinstate the death penalty. In the two years since the U.S. Supreme Court's decision abolishing the death penalty as cruel and unusual punishment, some in the North Carolina legislature have been trying to decide which crimes should bring the mandatory death sentence. From 1868 to April 1974, North Carolina had four capital offenses: first degree murder, forcible rape, first degree arson, and first degree burglary. The latter is quite unusual. First degree burglary is a property offense not involving direct personal contact and accounts for over two million crimes each year, which is 40 percent of the crime index total. In April 1974, the General Assembly modified capital offenses to include only first degree homicide and first degree rape. This occurred while thirty-three men, nearly half of all those awaiting the death sentence in the United States, awaited execution on death row at Central Prison.

North Carolina's record from 1910, when the state took over the task of executing condemned criminals, shows that 706 persons received the death sentence while 362, or slightly more than half, were actually executed (Table 7-1). Of those executed, 282 (78 percent) were black males, seventy-three (28 percent) were white males, and five (1 percent) were Indian males. Only two females have been executed, both of whom were black (North Carolina, 1972).

Two-thirds (twenty-two persons) of the thirty-three condemned to die in North Carolina as of May 1974 were black, one was an Indian male, and the only female was black. Blacks have been routinely screened off the juries in these capital cases. Further, seasoned trial lawyers are not assigned indigent capital cases, leaving the defense to "green" attorneys who often have just completed school. Sixteen of the twenty-two black defendants were considered indigent.

The North Carolina correctional system consists of seventy-seven facilities: one maximum security unit; three close custody units, including the correctional center for women; twenty-three medium security units; and fifty minimum custody facilities. The North Carolina state correctional system is unique in that both misdemeanors and felons are absorbed into the same system.

The state system has ten thousand inmates incarcerated in its institutions at any given time. This is high for a state with a population of five and a half million people, in contrast to the New York State correctional system (twenty-one institutions) which serves a state of over eighteen million people and only has 12,210 males and 369 female inmates (McKay, 1972).

In North Carolina, 9,776 persons were incarcerated in 1972 in the state correctional system. Of these, 97 percent were males and 3 percent were females. Within the male sample, 30 percent were imprisoned for misdemeanor charges and 70 percent for felony charges. Black males were overrepresented in the felony category comprising 41 percent of the male inmate total. Similarly, 26 percent of the females were sentenced for misdemeanor charges and 74 percent

Table 7-1
Death Sentences in North Carolina, 1910-1961

Offense	Total Sentenced	Not Executed	Those Executed
1. Murder	531	251	280
2. Rape	131	60	71
3. Burglary	41	30	11
4. Arson	3	3	0
Total	706	344	362

for felony offenses. The black female felon was overrepresented in the female sample, accounting for 50 percent of the female inmate total.

The data analyzed in this investigation include the total 1973 inmate population of the state's only maximum security unit and the only female facility, the Correctional Center for Women. Both are located in Raleigh, the state capital. Approximately 10 percent of those incarcerated are in the maximum security prison while the Correctional Center for Women accounts for about 300 inmates. The remainder are located in the other seventy-five institutions. Those incarcerated in either the maximum prison or the Correctional Center for Women are considered the most serious male and female offenders in the state. The two facilities differ considerably. The maximum security prison is an old structure, built in the last century. It is often overcrowded and lacks adequate ventilation. One wing is for serious felons, who are isolated from the more transient east wing population.

Overcrowded conditions, subcultural animosities, especially racial strife, and the lack of any universal token economy system for the inmates results in a high tension situation, one where the inmate is caught between staff and subcultural controls and demands. In the late 1960s a riot resulted in the death of eight inmates at the hands of the assault force. More recently, numerous inmates have been executed at the hands of other inmates.

Women's prison, in contrast, is a camp facility with dormitories and cottages on a campus-like estate surrounded not by walls, but by an uncharged fence. Most of the women work in either the sewing shop making all the uniforms for the prison system, or the laundry which services many of the surrounding public institutions.

The Findings

The racial distribution evidenced a wide discrepency in the racial composition within the two penal facilities as compared to that in the general state population. Among males in the state, 23 percent were black; yet the maximum security prison population of 806 consisted of 55 percent blacks. The female distribution within the state is 24 percent black, while 64 percent of the 292 women incarcerated at the Correctional Center for Women were black and 34 percent were white (Table 7-2).

Tables 7-3 and 7-4 provide a profile of the types of offenses for which these felons were incarcerated at either the maximum security prison or the Correctional Center for Women. Slightly less than 60 percent (474) of the males were incarcerated for personal offenses, those directly involving injury or threat of injury to another person, while 35 percent involved property offenses. Only 6 percent were nonvictim offenses. In contrast, 39 percent (115) of the females were incarcerated for personal crimes, 39 percent for property crimes, and 22 percent

Table 7-2
Inmate Distribution

Sex	White	Black	Total
Men	363 45%	443 55%	806
Women	99 34%	193 66%	292
Total	462 42%	636 58%	1,098

for victimless offenses. The implication here is that males are imprisoned largely for "violent offenses" while female incarcerations seem to be distributed more evenly across the three categories. An interesting difference is the 22 percent rate for "moral" charges (victimless offenses) among the female sample as compared to only 6 percent for males. Blacks, at both institutions, accounted for slightly higher proportions of personal offenses (63 percent black males, 54 percent white males; 43 percent black females, 33 percent white females) while

Table 7-3
Type of Offense: Men

Race	Personal	Property	Nonvictim	Total
White	201 54%	144 39%	26 7%	371
Black	273 63%	136 31%	26 6%	435
Total	474 59%	280 35%	52 6%	806

Table 7-4
Type of Offense: Women

Race	Personal	Property	Nonvictim	Total
White	33 33%	50 51%	16 16%	99
Black	82 43%	64 33%	47 24%	193
Total	115 39%	114 39%	63 22%	292

accounting for fewer property offenses (31 percent black males, 39 percent
white males; 33 percent black females, 51 percent white females).

Using the list of FBI Crime Index offenses as a guide, a more specific break-
down can be reported for both institutions. Those male inmates who were convicted of the violent offenses of murder, rape, and aggravated assault accounted
for 51 percent (270 offenders) of the Index offenses for the maximum security
prison sample and 32 percent of the institution's total male inmate sample
(806). The female sample, on the other hand, had only 34 percent (40 offenders)
of its Index crimes coming under the personal crimes of violence category, comprising 14 percent of the total female inmate sample (292). Black women were
credited with 61 percent of the total index offenses committed by women;
black males were responsible for 56 percent of the male index offenses.

The serious incarcerated felon population at the maximum security prison
and the Correctional Center for Women represent only a fraction of the state's
100,786 reported Index crimes for 1972, which consisted of 21,612 violent
offenses (murder, rape, and aggravated assault) and 79,174 property offenses
(robbery, burglary, grand larceny, and auto theft). The reported violent offenses
themselves account for over twice the entire incarcerated population in the state
correctional system, which includes many misdemeanors, questioning whether
with such a small percentage incarcerated if society is really protected from
criminally deviant behavior.

The educational data showed that 78 percent of the male and 82 percent of
the female sample had less than a high school education. The distribution across
racial lines, for both samples, was similar. Only 6 percent of both male and
female inmate population had any education beyond the high school level.

A similar pattern occurred regarding occupational status. The male sample
had 89 percent of its inmates falling within the lowest three categories of
Hollingshead's social position index. The entire female sample fell into these
categories. Forty percent of the black males occupied the lowest occupational
category compared to 25 percent of the white males while 62 percent of both
the black and the white female sample were from this category.

Together, the educational and occupational variables indicate that a considerable proportion of those incarcerated at both the maximum security
prison and the Correctional Center for Women were from the lower class irrespective of race, although a larger percentage of black males were from the
lowest occupational category than were white males.

Conclusion

Using the North Carolina Correctional system in general, and specifically two
correctional institutions as an example, some serious inconsistencies are illumi-
nated. It is apparent that the justice ideals of equal justice seem instead to be

noticeably selective, especially along class, race, and sex lines. Incarceration seems heavily influenced by these three variables in that there is a greater chance for a person who is poor, black, and male to be incarcerated in North Carolina prisons. The findings from this investigation clearly show that the majority of those incarcerated were black, on the lower economic level, and male.

This investigation does not look at those who were part of the attrition process that Sykes (1967) and others referred to; nor does it look specifically at judicial processes in North Carolina. In the absence of this information, one could possibly conclude that more blacks and poor commit crimes and subsequently are overrepresented in North Carolina's prisons. However, given the historical nature of North Carolina regarding the treatment of blacks, it would seem more plausible that the overrepresentation of blacks in prison is a result of the lingering effects of a dual system of justice. Certainly, Garfinkel's (1949) study of the racial attitudes of the North Carolina judicial system would add credence to this position. Other studies have shown that while whites may account for the majority of felony arrests, blacks appear to be adjudicated more harshly, accounting for the significant number of incarcerations. The overrepresentation of blacks in North Carolina's prisons is indeed consistent with many of the previous studies that have compared black with white inmates, which show that blacks tend to comprise a sizable percentage of the prison population.

The women in prison reflect the same discriminatory patterns found among their male counterparts regarding class and race. This analysis indicates that blacks and lower class females have an even higher percentage representation in the North Carolina correctional system than do the black males, even though the latter accounts for the greatest number of incarcerated persons in the state.

One other tentative conclusion that can be derived from this study of North Carolina's incarcerated population is that the criminal justice system has remained constant over a period of time. It seems apparent that the same type of prisoners who populated the prisons and chain gangs in the early North Carolina history still populate North Carolina's prisons today. The overrepresentation of blacks incarcerated which was noted in earlier studies continues to exist.

If this is so, then there is further reason to believe that the discriminatory justice as practiced earlier in history still exists. If the functions of America's judicial process do not facilitate or actualize its ideal mandate of equal justice, then what purpose does it serve and who benefits? A plausible answer focuses on the boundary-maintenance concept of relative justice and elitism. This perspective views justice and selective adjudication as being relative in that it is defined in line with the value system of those in control of society's main institutions, one that often is used to perpetuate the power differential between the "haves and the have nots."

References

Barnes, Harry and Negley Teeters. *New Horizons in Criminology*, 3rd ed. Englewood Cliffs, N.J.: Prentice-Hall, 1959.

Becker, Howard S. *Outsiders*. London: The Free Press of Glencoe, 1963.

Clark, Kenneth. *Dark Ghetto*. New York: Harper and Row, 1965.

Coser, Lewis. *The Functions of Social Conflict*. Glencoe, Ill.: The Free Press, 1956.

Dahrendorf, Ralf. *Essays in the Theory of Society*. Stanford, Calif.: Stanford University Press, 1968.

Douglas, Jack. *Deviance and Respectability*. New York: Basic Books, 1970.

Erikson, Kai T. *Wayward Puritans*. New York: John Wiley and Sons, 1966.

Garfinkel, Harold. "Research Note in Inter- and Intra-Racial Homicides." *Social Forces* 27 (1949): 381-396.

Ginzburg, Ralph. *100 Years of Lynchings*. New York: Lancer Books, 1962.

Goode, William J. "The Protection of the Inept." *American Sociological Review,* Feb. 1967, pp. 5-19.

Goode, Erich. "Marijuana and the Politics of Reality." *Journal of Health and Social Behavior,* June 1969, pp. 83-94.

Graham, Hugh and Ted Gurr. "Task Force on Historical and Comparative Perspectives." In *Violence in America*. New York: Bantam Books, 1970.

Gusfield, Joseph. *Symbolic Crusade*. Urbana: University of Illinois Press, 1963.

Kaplan, John. *Criminal Justice*. Mineola, N.Y.: The Foundation Press, 1973.

Kvaraceus, William and Walter Miller. *Delinquent Behavior*. Washington: National Education Association, 1976.

McKay, Robert. *Attica: The McKay Report*. New York: Bantam Books, 1972.

Merton, Robert. *Social Theory and Social Structure*. New York: The Free Press, 1966.

North Carolina, Department of Corrections. *North Carolina Death Row Statistics,* prepared by Adam Behre. Raleigh: by author, 1972.

Overby, Andrew. "Discrimination in the Administration of Justice." In Charles E. Reasons and Jack Kuykendall (eds.), *Race, Crime and Justice*. Pacific Palisades, Calif.: Goodyear Publishing Co., 1972, pp. 264-276.

Palmer, Stuart. *The Violent Society*. New Haven: College and University Press, 1972.

Pareto, Vilfredo. "The Circulation of Elites." In Talcott Parsons, Edward Shils, Kasper Naegele, and Jesse R. Pitts (eds.), *Theories of Society*. New York: Free Press, 1968.

Pound, Roscoe. *Social Control Through Law.* New Haven: Yale University Press, 1942.

President's Commission on Law Enforcement and Administration of Justice. *The Challenge of Crime in a Free Society.* Washington, D.C.: Government Printing Office, 1967.

Quinney, Richard. *Crime and Justice in Society.* Boston: Little, Brown and Co., 1969.

Quinney, Richard. *The Problem of Crime.* New York: Dodd, Mead and Co., 1970.

Rosenfeld, Gerry. *Shut Those Thick Lips.* New York: Holt, Rinehart and Winston, 1971.

Scheler, Max. *Resentiment.* New York: The Free Press, 1961.

Skolnick, Jerome. *The Politics of Protest.* New York: Ballatine Books, 1969.

Sykes, Gresham. *Crime and Society.* New York: Random House, 1967.

Steiner, Jesse and Roy M. Brown. *The North Carolina Chain Gang.* Chapel Hill: University of North Carolina Press, 1927.

U.S. Department of Justice, Federal Bureau of Investigation. *1972 Uniform Crime Report.* Washington, D.C.: Government Printing Office, 1973.

Wolfgang, Marvin. *Patterns in Criminal Homicide.* Philadelphia: University of Pennsylvania Press, 1958.

Part III

Black Crime: Offenders and Victims

8 Crime in the Black Community

Jimmy Bell and Irv Joyner

Statistical data, communal testimony, displeasured victims, and disoriented offenders attest to the rising crime rate in the black community. This crime rate is of such magnitude that many black community members have proclaimed a crime epidemic that threatens to reduce their community to a prison camp. According to Parker and Brownfield (1974), statistics released by the Federal Bureau of Investigation indicated that in 1971 blacks accounted for 66 percent of the reported arrests for robbery, 62 percent of the murders, 50 percent of the rapes, and 47 percent of the assaults. Despite the case that can be made for the clear distinction between reported offenses and conviction rates, it would seem that the black community has just cause for alarm.

Alarmed black citizens are raising questions, both publicly and privately. Why is crime on the increase in the black community? Who are the perpetrators? Who are the most likely victims? What must be done to reduce this deplorable trend? How can the citizens share in the responsibility of curtailing these dastardly acts? These questions reveal a tenseness in the black community that is justifiably replete with fear, anxiety, desperation, and disillusionment. Crime in the black community is rampant and the startling reality is that some blacks are robbing, assaulting, raping, and murdering other blacks in alarming proportions.

This chapter will attempt to examine some causal factors leading to crime and its escalation in the black community. Some speculations as to why blacks commit violence against other blacks will be discussed. Hopefully, some action programs presented in this dicussion will aid in the reduction of crime-related hardships in the black community. The trend of increasing crime rates must be reversed and necessary steps must be taken to motivate and mobilize community citizens to active resistence. In Harlem, a clergyman organized an armed militia and advised local residents to buy guns to protect themselves from what he termed "criminalization" (Parker and Brownfield, 1974). The Reverend Oberia D. Dempsey in 1967 proclaimed that a rising tide of crime had swept over the Harlem streets and that citizens feared to go out after dark. The muggers and robbers instilled panic among the people. Consequently, Mr. Dempsey organized a police militia that he called "Operation Interruption" with a membership approximately 2,600 strong, 200 of whom were active and armed (Parker and Brownfield, 1974). This seemingly extra-legal operation was legitimated by arming only those members who were eligible for or already had permits to carry guns. This tactic represents one extreme in community

69

self-protection; other communities have adopted more subtle policies and
practices which are appropriate for their situations.

Factors Contributing to Crime in the Black Community

Economics

The system of social stratification in this country tends to divide communities
into two general categories: those of economic affluency and those of economic
deprivation. Many behavioral scientists and laymen alike believe a correlation
exists between economic deprivation and crime. Deprivation is considered as a
precipitating, but not inclusive, cause of crime. Indeed, most citizens in the
black community are law abiding and do not engage in criminal activities. Who,
then, are the perpetrators? Perhaps some deprived individuals feel they are
trapped in a life and death struggle for survival in an affluent society where
wealth is very unequally distributed.
    Wolfgang (1964) convincingly points out that any child, black or white,
will feel oppressed if he enters a world offering rewards of status and success
which he cannot achieve. There is a moat of discrimination cutting him off
from the mainland, and few if any opportunities for him to achieve those
rewards. Economically deprived black children continue to wish for the same
things the mainlanders desire, but they are forced to move around a great deal, to
lose their fathers either by death or by desertion, or to lose their mothers to jobs
or through dependency. Additionally, Wolfgang suggests that deprived children
are given less knowledge to absorb and much less money than the mainlanders
receive for their tasks. He is surrounded with those who achieve rewards unlaw-
fully. He is made to protect the mainland, but prevented from participating in
making the rules to govern it. He is exposed to disease which shortens his life
span. Others call him racist names, treat him as if he were inherently inferior,
and convince him of his inferiority.
    What type of individual is likely to emerge from this? Such treatment sets
the stage for many unwholesome and upredictable events. Wolfgang implies
that the dominant American society has created these conditions which are,
perhaps, the explanations for the vast amount of crime and social disorder in this
country. Gaining access to the mainstream of American society may be an
impossible task for some in the black community, whose only available option
is a life of crime. Another speculation is that there are individuals who justify
careers in crime as a necessary evil to counteract years of oppression levied
against blacks by a white racist system. One of the most common notions
shared by black community dwellers is that offenders view crime as the
"American way"; it is much easier to take what is desired than to struggle trying
to earn a living. Certainly there are a multiplicity of variables relating to crime

causation. Economics, however, is a key variable which under careful analysis proves to be most significant.

Police Protection

Many citizens in the black community have questioned whether law enforcement officials are as zealous about providing the same or similar protection in black neighborhoods as compared to other communities. Kuykendall (1972) indicates that blacks view the police as representatives of an inequitable system and as an army of occupation. Blacks believe police do not adequately respond, if they respond at all, to complaints and that police either oppress or fail to provide sufficient protection. Kuykendall further states that many black community members feel that crimes involving only blacks are underenforced while black on white crime is overenforced. Indeed, many law enforcement agencies either covertly or overtly accept selective enforcement policies as standard procedure. This discretion to invoke the criminal process at will may be disasterous for entire segments of certain communities. It is logically sound to assume that the enormous and often dangerous amount of discretion enjoyed by individual police officers may and sometimes has lead to abuse. Consequently, many citizens in the black community view policemen as contributing to many criminal activities by condoning certain actions and ignoring others. Community members come to view the police as the enemy rather than the protector. Certainly such attitudes create an atmosphere of reciprocal mistrust and skepticism, thus causing very infrequent if any cooperation between the community and the police in attempts to solve the problems of crime.

Causes for the Increase of Crime

While the use of official criminal statistics to measure the incidence of criminality may not provide totally accurate information, many members of the black community will attest to the fact that there is too much crime in their communities. One possible cause is that unemployment rates are significantly higher among blacks than among whites in most occupational groups (U.S. Department of Commerce, 1974). Blacks are undergoing a period of economic austerity. Some blacks are permanently dropping out of the labor force, while others are systematically being forced out by layoffs, industrial relocation, etc. While unemployment may be a major precipitating cause of crime increase, Parker and Brownfield, (1974) insist that as economic conditions improve, crime rates increase rather than decrease. In any case, victims are easily accessible to the criminal.

The Perpetrators

There is a common belief that crime is committed by individuals residing outside the victim's community, but the individual engaging in criminal activity
may very well be one's neighbor. Conklin (1975) asserts that most felonies in
this country were committed by local residents rather than outsiders. Seventy-
eight percent of all arrests and more than nine of every ten juveniles arrested
were local residents. This would certainly make crime in the black community
very threatening since it occurs on a face-to-face and a day-to-day basis.

Individuals who have dropped out of the formal education process are
considered to be likely offenders. In fact, evidence suggests a definite correlation between low educational achievement and individuals presently incarcerated
in America's confinement system. Although official statistics are believed to
have political overtones, a cursory glimpse provides a profile of the typical
offender. Quinney (1975) reports that those committing violent crimes in
seventeen U.S. cities were twenty-five years old and under, white (24 percent),
and male (62.3 percent). One could speculate that the corresponding figures
for criminals in the black community would reveal that most are young black
males.

Black Youth and Crime

Black youth are responsible for a wave of crime in the black community. Once
again the pattern of economic deprivation usually is the contributing and precipitating force behind the acts of delinquency. High rates of unemployment
would appear to steer a black youth in the direction of criminal activity, coupled
with a desire to maintain peer group acceptance via dress, life-styles, and a
variety of "social happenings." Youth residing in extremely low income areas
are more likely to become victims of unfulfilled aspirations. Various forms of
media exposure tends to heighten the economically deprived youth's materialis-
tic consciousness. This especially applies to "blaxploitation" movies. Black
youth's contact with police officers have historically resulted in negative experiences. The consequence of such situations is that black youths are commiting
crimes. An effort toward value clarification for black youth is urgently needed
to restore pride and faith in black posterity.

The Victims

A survey of victims in Chicago in 1967 found that black males and females were
most likely to be the victims in crimes against persons. A black males is six times
more likely than a white male to be a victim. Black women are likely to be

victims eight times more often than white women. Blacks in Chicago are more likely to assault other blacks, and whites are most likely to assault whites (Parker and Brownfield, 1974). A similar survey in Washington, D.C., performed by a presidential commission (1966) found that only twelve of 172 murders were interracial. Eighty-eight percent of rape cases involved persons of the same race. Out of 121 aggravated assault cases identified, only 9 percent were interracial. Robbery cases, however, were found to be interracial; 56 percent of the cases involved black offenders and white victims (Parker and Brownfield, 1974). Crime patterns in other cities are believed to follow the same or a similar trend.

Citizen Involvement

It is quite obvious that crime is not only a police problem, but also a community problem. Many members of the black community feel compelled to share in the responsibility of reducing crime in their communities. Black citizens are volunteering in many communities across the country, organizing in concerted efforts to stamp out crime that threatens to disrupt, impede, and destroy the very core of black communities. Some community efforts to resist crimes are the following:

1. Community meetings are called to raise the level of community consciousness to active resistance. Meeting places are usually civic clubs, church gatherings, private homes, public schools, and anywhere else that dialogue may take place. The initial thrust must be to develop an organization.

2. One very strong measure is the organizing of "police militia" whereby individuals with permission to carry weapons for defense assist in an official capacity to reduce rising crime rates. It is suggested that before this method is undertaken some consultation be made with proper legal officials in order to define the community group's status.

3. Community block clubs are being formed to oversee and report suspicious conduct in the vicinity. This method does not necessarily subject the participant to potential harm, but does aid in solving crimes and promoting improved police-community relations.

4. Community anticrime centers are organized to work with local groups to implement community-controlled programs which combat crime and reduce the opportunity for crime to take place. This should include family crisis intervention, legal education, referral programs, youth activities, and a provision for community redress of their grievances against agents of the criminal justice system.

5. Citizen review boards are organized to monitor the activities of the criminal justice system (police, courts, and prisons); to receive and investigate citizen complaints; and to propose community, legislative, and legal actions to force changes within the criminal justice system.

6. Alternatives to incarceration are offered by community-based programs (not necessarily facilities) that provide meaningful optional enterprises for offenders, such as educational and employment opportunities.

7. Campaigns against repressive legislation include continual efforts to review all legislation and to mount community campaigns to prevent the passage of all repressive legislation, such as that dealing with capital punishment, wiretap authority, and indiscriminate search and seizure.

8. Drug hotlines are designed to identify and expose the suppliers and pushers of drugs throughout the community. Provisions should be set up to protect persons providing information against drug dealers in and out of the community. To be successful, a drug hotline must be supported by drug detoxication programs.

Conclusion

Crime is growing at alarming rates within the black community. The causes are various; the need for remedial action is great. No one approach can solve these problems. What is needed is an eclectic approach, involving improved relations between the community and the criminal justice system, a more sensitive and responsible criminal justice system, community-based action programs, education programs, victim-oriented programs, and economic improvement programs. A comprehensive approach, utilizing some of the actions outlined in this chapter, is essential if crime in the black community is to be alleviated.

References

Conklin, John E. *The Impact of Crime.* New York: Macmillan Publishing Co., 1975.

Kuykendall, Jack L. "Police and Minority Groups: Toward a Theory of Negative Contacts." In Charles Reasons and Jack Kuykendall (eds.), *Race, Crime and Justice.* Pacific Palisades, Calif.: Goodyear Publishing Co., 1972, pp. 219-235.

Parker, J.A. and Allen C. Brownfield. *What the Negro Can Do About Crime.* New York: Arlington House Publishers, 1974.

Quinney, Richard. *Criminology.* Boston: Little, Brown and Co., 1975.

U.S. Department of Commerce, Bureau of Census, Social and Economic Statistics Administration. *The Social and Economic Status of the Black Population in the United States, 1973,* Special Studies Series P-23, No. 48. Washington, D.C.: Government Printing Office, 1974.

Wolfgang, Marvin E. *Crime and Race.* New York: Institute of Human Relations Press, 1964.

9

Rape, Race, and Research

Patricia Evans

Rape. It seldom makes the front pages anymore. It always did when I was a little girl growing up on Frenchmen Street in New Orleans. At least, rape as it was known then got the best newspaper space. Somehow the stories were always the same—"Black Man Rapes White Woman." As white female children, we were soon taught to believe that rape, especially by a black man, was a fate worse than death.

Although Frenchmen Street was an artery of blacks and whites living side by side, the closest calls my two sisters and I had were not with black men. Once near the railroad tracks some white men unloading horses coaxed us behind the unloading ramp. We fled in terror as they attempted to lift up our dresses. Another time in the Famous Theater my sister was dragged out of the back door of the picture show by a white man too drunk to have all of his senses. And that alone saved her. In broad daylight it happened again. In front of a grocery a white man in a car exposed himself to us. By this time we had learned our lesson well—run.

It is different now. Somewhere between page two and the want ads there is a report that a woman has been raped. Until recently, rape was something seldom talked about. But the collusion of silence about rape has been broken. Talking about rape is now the thing to do. Television crime shows, talk shows, and even news shows deal with the subject. Even clubs and organizations discuss this problem.

Rape is one of the most brutal of all crimes. Rape victims need not be physically injured to suffer deep and lasting pain. Few crimes leave their victims with deeper psychic hurt. For a woman, rape is one of the most feared of all crimes. Only murder ranks higher. One rape spokesperson has suggested that short of homicide, rape is the ultimate violation of self. Surely no woman, black or white, can ever think about rape impersonally.

Both in and out of their homes women are vulnerable to rape. It has been said that women are always in someone else's territory once they leave their homes. Susan Griffin (1971) expresses the feeling of many women when she infers that from childhood to old age, women live with a basic fear that they can be raped. It was this fear that, as little girls, my two sisters and I were told we could not walk past those mysterious warehouses after dark. It was the reason that, if we came home from the movies after dark, we would dash the two blocks to our house after we debarked from the city bus. It was the reason we were forbidden to cut through an overgrown vacant lot on the way to the bakery around the corner. It was the reason we were told not to get too friendly with black male strangers. As little girls, fear of rape was a childhood burden. As adults, women retain the burden—the necessity of considering themselves potential rape victims.

This personal narrative about the phenomenon of rape describes the effect that the topic of sexual assault has had on many women in our society. However, rape and the attitudes that surround it affect everyone. The impact is so great that no investigation of the criminal justice system would be complete without some discussion of the crime that many women view with the greatest fear. In many respects, rape, at least in America, has been considered a black man's crime, especially since black men have been punished so severely for rape. This fact, in addition to causing some concern to black citizens, warrants further exploration. What causes the black man to become a rapist? How can the potential black rapist be identified? Do women provoke the black man to rape? Do black men rape white women more often than black women? Why has the black man been punished so severely for the act of rape? It is difficult to look at the racial aspects of rape without looking at rape in general, for the topic is shrouded in many half-truths and misconceptions.

Misinformation About Rape

Rape is a crime that has thrived on myth, prejudice, indifference, and on the silence of its victims and potential victims. It is a silence of shame. Although the number of rape cases is increasing faster than any violent crime, the number of rape cases resulting in arrest and conviction is proportionately very low.

It is the least reported of all crimes. Police estimate that as many as four out of five victims never report they have been raped. Some of the reasons for the silence are fear of vengeance, the police, courtroom hassles, and embarrassment. In addition to being ashamed, some women are afraid that they will not be believed. Many people, for example, still believe that the woman asked to be raped or that it is impossible for a woman to be raped without her consent or that a woman enjoys being raped. The facts concerning rape are just beginning to be sorted from the fantasies.

In 1971, *Patterns in Forcible Rape* by Menachem Amir was published. Based on the examination and evaluation of 646 rape cases in Philadelphia, Amir's study destroyed many myths about rape and provided new information on the subject. Perhaps the most common myth was the widely held belief that a rapist is a sexually unfulfilled man who is suddenly carried away by an uncontrollable surge of desire. Amir found premeditation present in 90 percent of the group rapes and in 58 percent of the rapes committed by one man. These findings suggest that contrary to popular belief, rape can be motivated by factors other than sex and is not a crime of passion but more so one of violence. The rape act is merely the chosen mode to express violence.

Another popular myth destroyed by Amir's investigation is that most women are raped in dark alleys or while hitchhiking. Amir found that one-third of all rapes are committed by a man who forces his way into a victim's home and that over half of all rapes occur in a residence. Furthermore, he found that 48 percent of the rapists were either casual friends or close relatives of the victim. His finding calls for a reexamination of the notion that the typical rapist is a stranger to the victim.

Another frequent misconception is that rape victims invite the rapists' assault by wearing provocative clothing and by looking attractive. In fact, provocation is often a factor which figures into the assailant's defense. The facts are, however, that many elderly women, simply dressed matrons, and nuns have been raped merely because they happened to be at a specific place at a specific time.

The case of a convicted rapist confined in Louisiana's Angola State Prison exemplified how little provocation figures in many rapes. The rapist admitted having sexually assaulted one woman per week for a period of fifteen years in the city of New Orleans. On a given morning, he would wait in his car in a suburban neighborhood until the husbands left for work, at which time he would approach a given house with a grey poodle. When a woman answered the door, he would ask her if she had lost a poodle and then forcibly enter the house and rape her. In spite of the obvious lack of provocation on the part of the house-wives, women like them are consistently harassed in courtrooms across the country by questions which imply that they must bear the responsibility for the crime committed against them.

Closely related to the strong belief that women are instigators in the rape is the conviction that many rape victims do not tell the truth. The concern of many as to whether the victim does or does not tell the truth is reflected in the FBI's Uniform Crime Reports under an "unfounded category." Rape cases can be considered "unfounded" when the physical evidence contradicts the victim's account of the offense or when there is other credible evidence indicating the falsity of a complaint. One study on rape and the victims of rape revealed that in some police departments, the rate of unfounded rape was as high as 25 percent (U.S. Department of Justice, 1975c). In 1975, the national average was about 15 percent (U.S. Department of Justice, 1976).

Many Americans also share the beliefs that rape is impossible without a woman's consent, and that women enjoy being raped. Others suggest that a man cannot rape a woman without her assistance. The truth is a rape victim has very little control over what happens to her. She is either overcome by force or she submits out of fear that her life will be in danger if she struggles.

The rape assault can make a woman feel dirty, degraded, and powerless. In some instances, her very life may be at stake. The impact of rape on its victim is expressed quite well by Bard and Ellis (U.S. Department of Justice, 1975b), who say that rape "has to be one of the most crisis laden situations that can be sustained, particularly since it occurs in the context of moral taboos which traditionally have surrounded the sex functions of the female." The victim's acute distress over violation of her person is compounded by an aware-ness of cultural myths about rape which leads to fears of how friends, relatives, husband, or boyfriends may react to her. It is not unlikely that these factors cause the victim to feel guilty for having surrendered under duress to a fate worse than death. Borges and Weis (1973) reported that the reaction of most women to rape is humiliation and dehumanization.

Since the act of rape can be so crippling and so debilitating to both the victim and her family, it is not surprising to find great hostility toward the rapist. Often the hostility is translated into severe consequences for the assailant. In the United States, 455 convicted rapists have been executed for the crime of rape (U.S. Department of Justice, 1975a).

Profile of the Rapist

"The typical American rapist might be the boy next door," according to Brownmiller (1975) in her book *Against Our Will: Men, Women, and Rape,* especially if the boy next door happens to be about nineteen years old and lives in the victim's neighborhood and if the neighborhood happens to be "lower class."

In making generalizations about the rapist, however, caution must be exercised with the interpretation of statistics since there are many acts of rape, few arrests, and still fewer convictions. Of all the rape cases reported to the police in cities with a population of 250,000 or more, a clearance rate of 50 percent was recorded. Of those arrested, only 58 percent were prosecuted for rape (U.S. Department of Justice, 1976).

In spite of the fact that much of the information about the rapist is un-known, there are some common elements which consistently emerge. Most researchers on the subject report that the majority of the offenders are young. Fifty-eight percent of the reported rapists were under the age of twenty-five and the largest concentration fell in the sixteen to twenty-four age group (U.S. Department of Justice, 1976). Blacks are disproportionately represented. According to the FBI, 49 percent of all those arrested for rape in 1972 were black (U.S. Department of Justice, 1973). In 1975, blacks comprised 45 per-cent of those arrested for rape (U.S. Department of Justice, 1976). Those arrested generally fall within the low socioeconomic level (Brownmiller, 1975). While this information is helpful, Amir's (1971) study of rape was the first source to provide a more detailed profile of the typical rapist.

It was revealed that he was an ordinary guy, with one exception. He was

more prone to violence. It was found that the rapist did not have a separate
pathology aside from what might characterize any offender who commits crime.
Other findings from Amir's data revealed that the rapist did not always act alone.
Forty-three percent of the rape cases were performed in pairs or groups. Generally, the typical rapists were not responding to spontaneous expressions of
uncontrollable lust, as more than half of the cases were planned. The typical
rapist was unaffected by the weather, as forcible rape increased only slightly
during the summer months; preferred weekend nights usually between 8 p.m.
and 2 a.m.; was likely to use physical force as a weapon; and was more likely to
rape a female of his own race.

Interracial Rapes

Historically and probably as a result of slavery in America, the black woman
has been exceptionally vulnerable to rape by white men. Even well into the
twentieth century, the susceptibility of the black female (without solid legal
recourse) to sexual assault by white men has been a legacy that many black
women have had to endure. Today many suspect that more white on black
rapes occur than are reported because white males have long had easy access to
black women with relatively little fear of being reported or punished. In fact,
Bowers (1973) inferred that no white man in the United States has been legally
executed for raping a black woman. Golden (1975) summarizes the sexual
attitudes centering upon black female sexuality by saying that black females
have been the instruments "by which white men and especially Southern
white men, through the act of rape have in the past proved their disdain for and
dominance over black men."
    While the black woman has had to contend with the ever present prospect
of being sexually assaulted by the white man, the black man has been the focal
point of interracial rapes. The concern for the black man and the rape act has
been expressed most vividly through the disproportionate number of blacks
legally executed for rape. Of all the 455 men legally executed in the United
States for rape from 1930 to 1964, 89 percent have been black (U.S. Department
of Justice, 1976). This figure does not include those blacks lynched by
vigilante action for rape or suspected rape prior to or during the same period.
That the black man has received severe penalties for being charged with raping
white women is an incontestable historic fact. However, in spite of increased
interest and more open discussions of rape, there still seems to be no clearer
understanding of black-white rapes than was known before.
    A paucity of facts make it difficult, if not impossible, to talk intelligently
about actual black-white rape cases or to make generalizations. The only
evidence which can be used to provide insight into this phenomenon is the
evidence of the records of black men convicted of rape who were lynched,

legally executed, or incarcerated. These indexes of black-white rape are so tainted by a traditionally dualistic justice system, racial prejudice, white woman purity, and other cultural and economic biases, that their validity in shedding light on the subject is at best questionable. For example, while women had to undergo a rigid examination to determine if she were lying with respect to an alleged white rapist, this was not the case generally when the accused was a black male. In many communities, the testimony of the white female would be adequate evidence that she was, in fact, raped. The famous case of the Scottsboro Boys of Alabama (Carter, 1973) accused of raping two white women adequately speaks to this issue. In a more recent but very similar case, three black men in Maryland were charged, convicted, and sentenced to death for the rape of a sixteen-year-old white girl, despite contradictory evidence by the alleged victim, exonerating evidence in the state attorney's office, and pleas of innocence by the defendants (Smith and Giles, 1975).

One interpretation of a high black on white rape execution figure centers on the white man's paranoia about black men. This line of thought has fostered the belief that the white male, in openly abusing and ravishing black women, became excessively fearful that the black man would retaliate by raping white women (Brownmiller, 1975; Griffin, 1971). Because of the fear of retaliation by the black man, the white woman became the symbol of virtue and purity, a being not to be touched by black men. In an effort to protect the white woman from suspected black male rape, the white man became overly sensitive to any false or real cases of rape by blacks. Therefore, the slightest suspicion of sexual interest by the black man for the white woman was met with swift processing and the severest punishment. Griffin (1971) notes that the myth of white purity and womanhood stimulated an unreasonable fear on the part of the white man of the black rapist and was used to justify the lynching and oppression of black men.

There has been a continuous search for an explanation in the makeup of the black man's social and cultural environment. These attempts have generally tried to establish a relationship between the black life-style and sexual aggressiveness. In some earlier accounts of ghetto male sexuality, within male street-corner life, great masculine prestige was allegedly attached to intercourse and the number of females one could attract (Liebow, 1967). This was translated to mean that a failure to have intercourse was a sign of failure as a man. This line of investigation leaves us with more questions than answers. Thus, nothing definitive is known about why some who live in ghetto areas become rapists and some do not; nor why those that do become rapists select white females as opposed to black females.

More recent investigation of black on white rapes has prompted highly speculative explanations which attempt to locate the cause in the changing perceptions of how blacks view themselves (Curtis, 1976). Using Eldridge Cleaver's retrospective analysis of why he raped white women in the early sixties (1968) as a focal point, this line of thought infers that cultural and racial identification (black pride, black awareness, and black power) has contributed to the lowering of internal restraints blacks previously had that prevented them from aggressing against whites. As a result, blacks are now more likely to attack the source of their frustration—which is considered to be white people. This view further supposes that because of these cultural factors, lower class blacks are more likely to rape white women than before. In addition to the lack of any empirical data, this fragile linkage between racial pride and rape is incomplete and inadequate as a viable explanation of the causes, for it still fails to help in distinguishing the rapist from the nonrapist. The viewpoint is so broad in scope that it is meaningless, for it identifies any and all black men in the ghetto who experience a black culture and racial identity as potential rapists of white women.

Another explanation proposed is the increased social interaction of white women with black men (Curtis, 1976). According to this line of reasoning, the liberalization of the white woman and the accessibility to black males increases her chances of becoming a rape victim.

While all these speculations are provocative and may, in varying degrees, be part of the total of the black rapist, there have been no consistent data that can be used to identify the black rapist who will rape white women from the black rapist who will rape black women, except after the rape act has occurred. In the final analysis, maybe there is no satisfactory explanation of why there is black on white rape or white on black rape.

The real issue is that the justice system not punish a man more or less severely because of his race or because of the race of the victim. The rape act is no less or no more painful or degrading to the victim whether she is white or black or whether the rapist is black or white and both black and white victims should receive equal access to the protection of the legal system.

And, just maybe, the media has adopted the best course of action. Instead of the heading "Black Man Rapes White Woman," the heading is "Woman Raped." The latter heading does not highlight the less important aspect of rape, which is color, but rather focuses on the real issues which are that a woman was involuntarily encroached upon and that women are still vulnerable to this dastardly act.

Intraracial Rape

In spite of the pronounced emphasis on the black man raping the white woman, the available evidence indicates that interracial rape acts are exceptionally small. A survey of seventeen cities and the use of 1967 police statistics revealed that only 10 percent of all reported cases were black on white rapes and less than 1 percent were white on black rapes (Curtis, 1974). Amir (1971) found that only 7 percent of the Philadelphia rapes were interracial. These studies show that reported rape is mostly a black on black, white on white phenomenon. Most of the data show that black females are the disproportionate victims of reported rapes. In Amir's study, at least 76 percent of the cases were black on black. Curtis (1974) reported that almost 60 percent of a national survey on rape involved black men raping black women.

The causes of all rape in general, and white on white rapes in particular, are explained typically by elements of sexual and aggressive urges in varying combinations. A rape act can be classified as the result of one of the following: displaced aggression, sexual urges, the coexistence of sexual urges and aggressive urges, impulse, or antisocial personality (Coleman, 1976).

Perhaps many black on black rapes can be attributed to one of the causes which explain white on white rape. However, explanations for the causes of other black on black rapes are typically more complex. Generally people search for an extra dimension to explain black rapes. For example, in addition to the causes listed above for intraracial rapes, the black rapist is generally described as being motivated by racial and/or cultural factors. The common themes are feelings of emasculation and powerlessness (Rader, 1973) and masculinity equated with sexual conquests (Liebow, 1967). Another interpretation of black on black rapes is the perception of the black man that it is safer to rape a black female and escape harsh punishment from the criminal justice system (Sutherland and Cressey, 1974).

The reasons proffered to explain black on black rapes certainly seem to be congruent with the sociocultural environment experienced by the black male. However, the question remains unanswered as to why some blacks from the same environment become rapists and some do not. Clearly there is a need to conduct more extensive research on the black rapist. Present research indicates that there is no typical black rapist. Golden (1975) suggests that the main difference between the rapist and the nonrapist is, "a mature, healthy attitude towards women and an ability to control anger and sexual impulses."

Help for Rape Victims

There is no longer a need for the rape victim to feel that she cannot be helped after suffering the painful event of a rape. In many cities, rape crisis centers offer help to rape victims. There are about 140 such centers currently operating offering a variety of services, such as supportive services to victims, education programs to the public on rape-related issues to reform the law. Personnel in these centers believe that women can benefit from sharing their experiences and feelings with each other. Most staff members feel that the sense of helplessness often resulting from a rape can be overcome in part by giving a victim the opportunity to regain control of herself, rather than by having someone else take care of her. They generally offer a victim whatever support services and information that are necessary to meet her needs, as she defines these needs.

In addition to the obvious need for rape crisis centers in minority communities where large percentages of rapes occur, there is a need for more female law enforcement officers, especially black female law officers because this initial contact with the criminal justice system is critical.

Conclusion

Even though sexual assault is as old as history, there is still a myriad of unknowns about the subject. More research is clearly warranted on this old crime. However, in order to begin to seriously separate fact from fiction about rape, each criminal justice component needs to evaluate its complicity in maintaining the present state of affairs with regard to rape, including fear of reporting, myths, indifference, the accelerating rate of rape, and racial discrepancies. Rape must be recognized for what it is. By legal definition it is a crime of violence against females by males. Rape has been set in motion by the keepers of the power who have established the themes of behavior for the four main characters: black male, black female, white female, and white male. It has been a theme of sexual exploitation that needs to be amended.

References

Amir, Menachem. *Patterns in Forcible Rape.* Chicago: University of Chicago Press, 1971.

Borges, Sandra and Kurt Weis. "Victimology and Rape: The Case of the Legitimate Victim." *Issues in Criminology* 8 (1973): 71-115.

Bowers, William J. *Executions in America.* Lexington, Mass.: D.C. Heath and Company, Lexington Books, 1973.

Brownmiller, Susan. *Against Our Will: Men, Women and Rape.* New York: Simon and Schuster, 1975.

Carter, Dan T. *Scottsboro.* New York: Oxford University Press, 1973.

Cleaver, Eldridge. *Soul on Ice.* New York: McGraw Hill, 1968.

Coleman, James C. *Abnormal Psychology and Moden Life,* 5th ed. Glenview, Ill.: Scott, Foresman and Co., 1976.

Curtis, Lynn A. *Criminal Violence: National Patterns and Behavior.* Lexington, Mass.: D.C. Heath and Company, Lexington Books, 1974.

Curtis, Lynn A. "Rape, Race and Culture: Some Speculations in Search of a Theory." In Marcia J. Walker and Stanley L. Brodsky (eds.), *Sexual Assault.* Lexington, Mass.: D.C. Heath and Company, Lexington Books, 1976.

Golden, Bernette. "The Ugly Crime of Rape." *Essence,* June 1975, p. 36.

Griffin, Susan. "Rape, the All-American Crime." *Ramparts,* 10 (1971): 26-35.

Liebow, Elliot. *Tally's Corner.* Boston: Little Brown and Co., 1967.

Rader, Dotson. "The Sexual Nature of Violence." *New York Times,* Oct. 22, 1973, p. 31.

Smith, Robert and James V. Giles. *An American Rape: A True Account of the Giles-Johnson Case.* Washington, D.C.: The New Republic Book Co., 1975.

Sutherland, Edwin H. and Donald R. Cressey. *Criminology,* 9th ed. Philadelphia: J.B. Lippincott Co., 1974.

U.S. Department of Justice, Federal Bureau of Investigation. *1972 Uniform Crime Reports.* Washington, D.C.: Government Printing Office, 1973.

U.S. Department of Justice, Federal Bureau of Investigation. *1975 Uniform Crime Reports.* Washington, D.C.: Government Printing Office, 1976.

U.S. Department of Justice, Law Enforcement Assistance Administration, National Criminal Justice Information and Statistics Service. *Capital Punishment 1973.* National Prisoner Statistics Bulletin SD-NPS-CP-2, Washington, D.C.: Government Printing Office, 1975a.

U.S. Department of Justice, Law Enforcement Assistance Administration, National Institute of Law Enforcement and Criminal Justice. "Crisis Intervention and Investigation of Forcible Rape," prepared by Morton Bard and Katherine Ellis. In *Rape and Its Victims: A Report for Citizens, Health Facilities, and Criminal Justice Agencies,* edited by Lisa Brodyaga and Margaret Gates, pp. 166-171. Washington, D.C.: Government Printing Office, 1975b.

U.S. Department of Justice, Law Enforcement Assistance Administration, National Institute of Law Enforcement and Criminal Justice. *Rape and Its Victims: A Report for Citizens, Health Facilities, and Criminal Justice Agencies.* Edited by Lisa Brodyaga and Margaret Gates. Washington, D.C.: Government Printing Office, 1975c.

10

Black Women: Income and Incarceration

Eleanor Saunders Wyrick and *Otis Holloway Owens*

Introduction

Prison inmates are increasingly female. Between 1971 and 1974 the rate of increase for women incarcerated in state (15.6 percent) and federal (25.2 percent) prisons exceeded that of men with 12.2 percent and 2.0 percent respectively (U.S. Department of Justice, LEAA, 1976). The total female inmate population consisted of federal (4 percent) and state (3 percent) prisoners. The data show that the percentage of females in federal institutions had increased to 7 percent by 1976 (U.S. Department of Justice, Bureau of Prisons, 1976a). Undoubtedly these percentage increases reflect the growing trend for women to commit more serious crimes.

Adler (1975) reports increases between 1960 and 1970 in female arrests for robbery (277 percent, embezzlement (303 percent), and burglary (168 percent). These figures were significantly higher than increases for men. The National Advisory Commission on Criminal Justice revealed female recidivism was reaching crisis proportions. The number of women with one or more commitments was 21 percent higher in 1973 than in 1967 (U.S. Department of Justice, 1974a). The data show an increase of 73 percent for the general female offender population committed from the courts (i.e., probation or other community-based correctional services), to federal institutions (U.S. Department of Justice, FBI, 1973).

Prison inmates are increasingly black. Despite the fact that blacks account for only 11 percent of the U.S. population, they comprise 35 percent of the federal prison population and 47 percent of the state prison population. A closer analysis of the prison population has also shown that, proportionate to the total population, the black female remains overrepresented. In 1970, black women made up just under one-half (48.8 percent) of all women eighteen years old and older in state prisons (5,497). According to Foster, over half of the federal female prisoners were black in 1974 (U.S. Department of Justice, 1974a) and the fact remains the same in 1976 (U.S. Department of Justice, Bureau of Prisons, 1976).

The proportion of blacks to non-black women incarcerated in certain states exceeds 50 percent. For example, blacks total a little less than two-thirds of the women over age eighteen that are incarcerated in the Women's Detention Center (WDC) in the District of Columbia. In this same institution, three-quarters of all first bookings were blacks. Further, 83 percent of the women who returned to the WDC from initial court hearings were black. An overwhelming

percentage (92 percent) of those sentenced for thirty or more days were black
(McArthur, 1974). In Alabama, black women represented 75 percent of the
approximately 185 women incarcerated in state prisons (Center, 1973).

Income and Incarceration: A Tenacious Bond

There are pronounced parallels between the black female labor market and
the low economic profiles of black female offenders. Foster reported in her
study of the female offender that prior to incarceration nearly two-thirds of
the residents at the Federal Correctional Institution, Alderson, West Virginia,
earned less than $3,000 per year. An additional 20.4 percent earned less than
$5,000 per year. Another study Foster conducted for the Alderson staff
revealed that approximately 30 percent of all women inmates were on welfare
before incarceration (U.S. Department of Justice, 1974a). The low earnings
of black women may be related to the high percentage of black women
employed as household domestics and in other low skill and low pay occupations.

   Related in no small way to the economic status of the black female
offender and prisoner are age, education, and marital status. The black female
offender tends to be young and undereducated. The largest number of black
females fall within the eighteen- to twenty-five-year-old group. In contrast,
white females tend to cluster in the twenty-six- to thirty-five-year-old category.
With few exceptions, the education level of female prisoners ranged from
grades five to ten. Most were single (U.S. Department of Justice, 1974b).

   The low or no income status of the female offender is even more crucial
when one considers that she is also likely to have dependent children. A study
of Alderson residents showed that most (66.1 percent) had dependent
children. A study of the women in Pennsylvania jails revealed that 80 percent
were mothers of dependent children (McArthur, 1974). These data are alarming when viewed with the understanding that these children are most likely to
be living in single parent and/or low income families.

   According to a special study conducted in 1973, three times as many
black children (43 percent) as white children (14 percent) live in families
where the father is absent, unemployed, or out of the labor force. Of some
2.9 million black children in fatherless families, nearly 40 percent were
supported on less than $3,000 per year. Another third were in the next broad
income group earning less than $5,000 (U.S. Department of Labor, 1973).
Only a third of the black women who head families had at least a high school
education. The economic status of black women does not appear to be improving as black unemployment continues to more than double the latest nationwide
unemployment statistics of 7.9 percent. Typically, the rate of employment for
black women surpasses that of black men.

The Urban League has developed a "hidden unemployment index" which places the figure for black unemployment at 25.4 percent. The League's index includes, in addition to persons actively looking for work, those not in the labor force who want a job now and all part-time workers who want full-time jobs. The League's study shows an astonishing unemployment rate of 64 percent among black teenagers in poverty areas (Patterson, 1976). Unemployment is highest among the black female teenager, which may lead to an early introduction of crime.

It is not surprising that black females are most frequently incarcerated for crimes that are economically related. According to a 1973 Federal Bureau of Prisons report of female offenders, there were 392 persons in the "all other" category (this means mostly black). Of this number, 196 were convicted of theft, forgery or larceny. The next largest group of convictions was related to drug offenses, many of which were economically motivated. The U.S. Bureau of Prison figures show that black females were sentenced an average of 5.4 years for all offenses and that offenders generally serve only about half of their sentences. This translates to an average of about 2.7 to three years (U.S. Department of Justice, 1974b). Any rehabilitative efforts for the black female offender should consider the factors of age (18-25) and the economic nature of their offenses.

Except for the added burden of the "ex-con" label, there is no difference between the before and after economic needs of the black female offender. They usually go to jail because they are broke and they often return to jail because they are still broke. Obviously, it is of great importance for the released offender to identify a source of income if she is to survive on a day-to-day basis. According to a special task force investigating post-arrest drug traffic, the second largest number of drug violation repeaters are in the twenty- to twenty-four-year-old bracket (U.S. Department of Justice, DEA, 1974). Since it has already been demonstrated that black women offenders are usually eighteen to twenty-five years old and that drug offenses are the second biggest reason for their incarceration, a guarded verification of a trend toward recidivism among black females can be made.

When the incarcerated black female offender is released it is highly unlikely that she will be employed in a job where she can earn sufficient pay to take care of herself and her children. Thus, it is easy to predict her reversion to crime.

Improving Training Programs

Greater responsiveness to the needs of the black female offender can be achieved only if improvements are made in both rehabilitative services and vocational training. Effective vocational training should include the following: (1) preparation for jobs that pay substantially more than the minimum wage, (2) programs that can be completed within two and a half to three years, and (3) training for jobs geared to the vocational interests and physical energy levels of eighteen to twenty-five year olds. Sadly, present vocational rehabilitative efforts only tend to reinforce past economic failures.

At the present time most training programs offer little more than preparation for low status and low paying jobs including clerking, cooking, and domestic services. They command, at best, only minimum wages and benefits, offering doubtful opportunities for promotion (Leiberg and Parker, 1974). Other courses frequently offered are photography, plastics, and keypunching. These courses provide more favorable opportunities. However, employment in photography offers at the most a minimum wage job in a film development firm unless the student has an opportunity to serve as an apprentice to a master. Except for the limited number of craftsmen who design and made the injection molds, jobs in plastics are restricted to assembly line work for which minimum wages are paid. While keypunching holds pay possibilities above minimum wages, training is too often conducted on outmoded equipment. Jobs which pay low wages, provide no upward mobility, and offer limited job satisfaction are unlikely to induce lawbreakers to give up crimes which may be more lucrative.

There are at least two job training models that provide potential value in education of women. First, the U.S. Navy and the Federal Prison Industries jointly administer a keypunch program at Alderson, West Virginia, and Terminal Island, California (both federal correctional institutions housing women). Through this program, inmates learn and practice a viable skill with an error rate of one-half of 1 percent. This low error rate exceeds the standards of many commercial businesses. The California Institute for Women in Frontera offers a state-certified Licensed Practical Nurses training course and a cosmetology course geared to the California State Cosmetology Examination.

While such training is indeed beneficial, there is also a need for more women to be trained for nontraditional jobs, the better paying jobs usually reserved for men. The Model Cities Program in Jessup, Maryland, for example, funded a trade union cooperative program in welding for the residents of the Women's House of Corrections (McArthur, 1974). Other job possibilities could include bricklaying, carpenters' helpers, locksmiths, cabinetmakers, painters, furriers, small appliance repair, and typewriter repair. Oil field work, especially in the oil producing states including Texas, Louisiana, and Oklahoma, is another area of potential for black women. The training pay for these jobs exceed journeyman pay in many of the traditional jobs. Most of the registered apprenticeship programs require that the trainee be eighteen to twenty-one and have a high school diploma or General Equivalency Diploma (GED). This required age range for apprentices coincides with the ages of most black female offenders. Also, the time required for completing training programs is compatible with the average incarceration period. Most training programs could be accomplished or well underway during the average three-year period of incarceration.

Application of the nontraditional jobs concept must take into account the fact that many women will have to be aided in moving to places where there are jobs. Two American Indian women joined Exxon Pipeline Company as pipeliner beginners. One of the women earned $1.80 per hour in a former secretarial job. As a pipeliner beginner, she earned $4.31 an hour with time and a half on weekends. After six to twelve months she could possibly be promoted to a pipeliner earning $4.71 an hour. This placement, however, required relocation, which takes money. Reimbursing prisoners a fair share for labor performed and some adaptation of profit-sharing are two ways for prisoners to increase their "gate" money. A very important consideration is the transition of the incarcerated to freedom. Prison industry wages range from nothing in some states to $2.40 a day in Iowa. Females received approximately $753 each in one federal prison industry project. Administering such a program would provide those who wish to pursue bookkeeping or banking careers with practical experience ("Women," 1973).

Job placement assistance and follow up services are vital during the relocation process. Community groups including sororities, fraternities, churches, ministerial alliances, black bar associations, coalitions of black social workers, and other black-oriented community organizations provide possible sources of sponsors for halfway houses, referral services, emergency loans, housing, and meals. The Women's Component of Employ-Ex, and ex-offender program based in Denver, is an adaptation of the halfway house concept. The primary objective of this program was to provide employment and other supportive services vital to female ex-offenders in their reentry into society.

Increasing Women in the Correctional Work Force

The time is also long overdue for a careful examination of the assumptions and biases that have excluded women from most positions in corrections and enforcement. Agencies must take a careful look at the work to be performed for each occupational category in their system to see if sex alone constitutes a bona fide occupational qualification. In most cases it does not.

Women account for only 12 percent of the correctional work force. Of thirty-four institutions for women offenders listed in the 1971 American Correctional Association Directory, twenty-six were headed by women. In all the federal correctional institutions few women have been employed as warden and associate warden. Correctional officers constitute the largest number of federal female correctional employees, and the majority work in adult and juvenile institutions for female offenders. In most state and federal institutions for males, the only women employees are clerks and secretaries. Since correctional institutions usually select supervisors and administrators from the ranks, the fact that institutions for males are much larger has effectively eliminated most women from supervisory and administrative positions (National Advisory Commission, 1972).

The shortage of women in the work force can be seen in other areas of employment within the criminal justice system. Of 668 state, federal, and municipal agencies participating in a Police Foundation survey, 47 percent said that female police personnel were not used in the same capacity as males. Thirteen percent admitted that no advanced positions were available to females. Responses revealed a per agency average of 3.4 females in supervisory/command ranks. Most were in juvenile, community relations, records, and communications. There were about 500 "minority" women employed as police personnel—an average of one per responding agency (Eisenberg et al., 1973). A total of 497 black female attorneys constituted only 8 percent of all black lawyers (Epstein, 1973).

It is important to note that little is known about who is employed by the criminal justice system. In order to gain more information, the Law Enforcement Assistance Administration (LEAA) awarded Howard University a grant to study the recruitment and retention of minority correctional employees. Congress mandated a national planning study of personnel and planning needs for the criminal justice system.

While black women are overrepresented among the numbers of incarcerated women, they are underrepresented in the correctional work force. One way to remedy the imbalance is to increase the number of black women in the correctional work force. The most obvious way to accomplish this is by increasing the number of women in education and training programs. Thus, more historically black colleges and universities must offer criminal justice courses or degrees.

In the past, criminal justice careers lacked visibility in both black schools and the black community. Further, judging from the dearth of black criminal justice workers, the established criminal justice programs on white campuses have not been very visible to many black students. The organization of a consortium of black institutions, Positive Futures, Inc., may serve to alleviate the problem of too few black workers in corrections.

This consortium has an objective of establishing a bachelor's level degree in the field of criminal justice at nine historically black colleges by 1977. Females comprise about 40 percent of those participating in the developing criminal justice programs at the nine institutions (Williams, 1976).

The changes needed can be effected as more black females are routed away from education and humanities majors and into curricular that can prepare them for careers in law. Black women can contribute as policewomen, trainers, personnel officers, equal employment opportunity specialists, border patrol agents, lawyers, judges, para-legals, intelligence specialists, detectives, security guards, correctional officers, psychologists, administrators, juvenile detention counselors, roving youth leaders, and probation officers. Careers are also available as federal special agents with the Treasury, Drug Enforcement Administration, Central Intelligence Agency, FBI, Secret Service, and Customs.

Through the cooperative efforts of criminal justice agencies and educational institutions, student internships have been made available. One example is the cooperative education program sponsored by the Drug Enforcement Administration and Howard University. Students complete course requirements for the Bachelor of Arts or Master of Arts degree in criminal justice and spend the last semester of their senior year on the Drug Enforcement Administration payroll while learning to be undercover narcotics agents. After graduation and an additional six months of training, these trainees are eligible for permanent full-time positions without going through the red tape of civil service registers.

More black female ex-offenders must be hired by government agencies, correctional institutions, and police departments. This will necessitate liberalizing the interpretations of background investigations and security clearances that assume that well-compensated and meaningfully employed ex-offenders are more subject to temptation than are other employees.

Conclusion

The reasons why certain people commit crimes remains a highly complex phenomenon. It appears that especially for black women there is a solid relationship between income and incarceration. It seems ironic that prison rehabilitation training programs may actually increase recidivism by training incarcerated women for poverty level jobs. The problem is further complicated by the unending circle of dependents who are destined for a life of crime and incarceration. A commitment to cooperation is essential among the countless agencies in the actual training and follow up of those formerly incarcerated.

References

Adler, Freda. *Sisters in Crime.* New York: McGraw-Hill Book Co., 1975, pp. 133-154.

Center for Correctional Psychology and Alabama Law Enforcement Planning Agency. *Corrections in Alabama: A Master Plan.* University, Alabama: Department of Psychology, The University of Alabama, 1973, pp. 1, 11-13.

Eisenberg, Terry; Deborah Kent; and Charles R. Wall. *Police Personnel Practices in State and Local Governments.* Washington, D.C.: Police Foundation, 1973.

Epstein, Cynthia Fuchs. "Black and Female: The Double Whammy." *Psychology Today* 7 (1973): 57.

Flynn, Edith E. "The Special Problems of Female Offenders." Paper presented at the National Conference on Corrections, Chicago, 1972.

Leiberg, Leon, and William Parker. *The Mutual Agreement Program with Vouchers: An Alternative for Institutionalized Female Offenders.* College Park, Md.: American Correctional Association, 1974.

McArthur, Virginia A. *From Convict to Citizen.* Washington, D.C.: District of Columbia Commission on the Status of Women, 1974.

National Advisory Commission on Criminal Justice, *National Standards and Goals for Corrections.* Washington, D.C.: Government Printing Office, 1972.

Patterson, Pat. "Black Unemployment." *Black Enterprise* 7 (1976): 53-59, 75.

U.S. Department of Justice, Bureau of Prisons. *Female Offenders in the Federal Correctional System,* prepared by Euphesenia Foster. Washington, D.C.: Government Printing Office, 1974a.

U.S. Department of Justice, Bureau of Prisons. *Statistical Report, Fiscal Year 1973.* Washington, D.C.: Government Printing Office, 1974b.

U.S. Department of Justice, Bureau of Prisons. *Population Profiles Excluding Detentioners.* Washington, D.C.: Government Printing Office, 1976.

U.S. Department of Justice, Drug Enforcement Administration, Committee on Post-Arrest Drug Trafficking. *Report on Post-Arrest Drug Trafficking.* Washington, D.C.: Government Printing Office, 1974.

U.S. Department of Justice, Federal Bureau of Investigation. *Crime in the United States, 1972.* Washington, D.C.: Government Printing Office, 1973.

U.S. Department of Justice, Law Enforcement Assistance Administration. *Sourcebook of Criminal Justice Statistics, 1974.* Washington, D.C.: Government Printing Office, 1975.

U.S. Department of Justice, Law Enforcement Assistance Administration. *Prisoners in State and Federal Institutions on December 31, 1974.* Washington, D.C.: Government Printing Office, 1976, pp. 1-3.

U.S. Department of Labor, Bureau of Labor Statistics. "Burden of Support Falls More Heavily on Black Mothers," prepared by Anne M. Young. *Monthly Labor Review,* April 1973, pp. 37-40.

Williams, Hallen, Director, Criminal Justice Program, Positive Futures, Inc., Washington, D.C. Telephone interview, Dec. 1976.

"Women Employed as Pipeliners at Longview." *The Liner,* April 1973.

Part IV

Answers and Actions

11 Prison Education: Perspectives Past and Present

C. Schweber-Koren

Prison education has become so integral to the correctional process that current researchers do not ask whether an education program exists, but rather what kind, who are the instructors and the students, and what are the costs, benefits, and needs (Dell'Apa, 1973; McCollum, 1973). Most prison constituencies, including reformers, inmates, correctional and legislative representatives, agree that educating inmates is a worthwhile part of the correctional commitment. Quality education is essential if the inmate is to be returned to society with employment training and coping skills, areas of weakness which often help send persons to prison.

At present there are about 250,000 persons incarcerated in the United States, excluding those in local jails. About 10 percent are in the federal system. Blacks account for 35.6 percent of the federal population. Of these, 93 percent are black men and almost 7 percent are black women. Black women slightly outnumber all other female inmates (U.S. Department of Justice, 1976c). Table 11-1 shows the numerical and percentage distribution of black inmates compared with non-blacks.

The task of providing education to all segments of the prison population is indeed a monumental challenge. With this frame of reference, this investigation will look at correctional education programs with a focus on the black inmate. Specifically, education in adult institutions will be investigated by examining those programs reported to be among the best—the programs in the federal prisons (Roberts, 1971; Dell'Apa. 1973).

History

The education of prisoners is currently called correctional education. Its basic function as an agent of socialization and rehabilitation has not changed since its first introduction alongside the religious reformation of the nineteenth century (Lekkerkerker, 1931). Education has, however, altered considerably in form and scope since those first Bible lessons. The transformation occurred in three major chronological stages. In the early period (1798-1890), education

The author acknowledges with thanks the assistance of the staff of the Research Department, Federal Bureau of Prisons (Washington, D.C.) and Ron Phillips, staff member of the National Prison Project and former inmate.

Table 11-1
Federal Inmates by Race and Sex, 1976

	Men		Women		Total	
	Number	*Percent*	*Number*	*Percent*	*Number*	*Percent*
Black Inmates	8,487	33.2	622	2.4	9,109	35.6
Non-Black Inmates	15,865	62.0	589	2.3	16,454	
Total					25,563 all inmates	

Source: U.S. Department of Justice, Bureau of Prisons. "Population by Race". *Population Profiles Excluding Detentioners on June 30, 1976.* Computer Printout, 1976.

was a by-product of the reforming process, and teaching some reading and writing fit in with the notion that criminals could be saved by studying the Bible and obtaining its guidance. In the reformatory period (1870-1930), convicts were to be differentiated from each other and reform programs geared to the individuality of the newcomers. In this climate, education, especially literacy, became part of the reform concept since it could be used to instill discipline, combat idleness, and transfer substantive knowledge. In the modern period (1931-present), education became accepted as an integral part of the rehabilitative process. Some prisons began to look to educational developments outside for contacts and adaptations (Lekkerkerker, 1931; Roberts, 1971).

The belief in individualized treatment, in reform rather than retribution, led some to desire a special system for those criminals most likely to be reformable—the young and the women. These institutions were called reformatories. Brockway's work with young men at Elmira, and that of Jessie D. Hodder in Massachusetts and Margaret Elliot in Indiana with women, represent contemporary efforts in the states. The federal counterparts opened fifty years later: Alderson (West Virginia) for women in 1928 and Chillicothe (Ohio) for men in 1926 (Lekkerkerker, 1931). In all of these, the optimism that a person's antisocial behavior could change was inextricably linked with education as change agent. The system was operationalized by a classification process which examined each inmate's background, intellectual potential, and vocational needs, and then designed a program for obtaining the psychological and practical skills deemed necessary for that person to live in a free society. Although the reformers were more kindly toward convicts than their predecessors, it is sometimes difficult to distinguish the arrogance from the compassion. In committing themselves to fit the punishment to the criminal rather than the crime, reformatory advocates and practitioners set themselves up as the experts who decided what the reformed person should be. The perceptions were constrained by societal limits, so that females might be trained to sew or blacks to work in laundries (Lekkerkerker, 1931; National Committee, 1927). Inasmuch as education was inseparable from retraining, education's role expanded in this period to the point that it was a theoretically accepted part of the reforming process.

Education became a working part of corrections during the modern period. Subsequent activity dealt not with legitimation but with developing the different aspects, such as academic or social, in conjunction with the treatment model which dominated penal theory. This period is dated from 1930 with the public dissemination of Austin H. MacCormack's (1931) survey of correctional education. He concluded that in spite of the education work done by the major reformatories, most prisons were unaffected. MacCormack made recommendations that prison education include a comprehensive program of academic, vocational, social, and cultural activities. He argued in favor of individual instruction, fostering inmate participation on the basis of interest rather than force, a diverse curriculum for the varied inmates and avoidance of routine and stereotypic programming. Also, MacCormack saw inmate education as adult education and not the presentation of juvenile instruction to grownups.

The Federal Bureau of Prisons was established May 1930, and all federal prison institutions became part of this central administrative agency. The federal prison system adopted early the philosophy which recognized education as an important ingredient in prison rehabilitation although little beyond minimal academic instruction to eliminate illiteracy existed until the late 1930s (U.S. Department of Justice, 1976b). Vocational training was a corollary to the establishment of Federal Prison Industries in 1934. This nonprofit government corporation was to provide products and services for other federal agencies. Therefore, prison industries could provide inmates with work experience while fostering the creation of trade related training programs. In this process, vocational training was legitimized to the point of institutionalization. Within the next few years, instructors and librarians were added to some staffs, programs to prepare inmate teachers started, correspondence and cell-study options initiated. The Bureau of Prisons annual report for the mid-1930s stated that the demand for education was always greater than the availability of staff and facilities. About 60 percent of all federal prisoners were enrolled in some course (Roberts, 1971).

By the 1950s, some state and federal institutions developed linkages with state education departments in order to establish accredited prison programs and provide legitimate diplomas. According to research by Roberts (1971), education included literacy skills in a broader program to raise the educational level and marketability of the inmate upon release. Vocational programs diversified and increased. Courses such as typewriter repair, auto mechanics, radio shops, printing, IBM operators, and garmet workers were sometimes matched with trade instruction classes on theory, business math and science, drafting and mechanical drawing.

The extent to which this training actually enabled inmates to find employment or bypass union restrictions continues to be debated (Michael, 1968). The initial linking of vocational programs to prison industries, and thus systemwide needs, has meant that programs which are necessary for the system but not inmates may remain as one of the dominant and financially rewarding activities. For example, the garment factory at Alderson makes clothes and flags for the federal government. The inmates complain that this is not an employable skill. However, keypunching and work in the garment factory are sought after because they are the highest paying jobs. More recently, co-correctional institutions, with their concurrent male and female populations, have had to deal with eliminating sexual barriers to vocational programs, such as allowing women in welding and men in typing. The extent to which this occurs, and the support that the pioneers receive, remains to be explored.

In the past fifteen years, relationships with postsecondary institutions have been initiated to provide college level courses for capable and deserving inmates. The schools usually provide the instructor, sometimes the books and materials as well, or make arrangements for evaluating correspondence work (Roberts, 1971). In 1965, work and study release was adopted whereby selected inmates could leave the institution on a daily basis to jobs or schools in the community.

This historical synopsis of correctional education does not assume these developments affected all inmates, black or white, equally. There is considerable evidence that analyses of aggregate populations often describe the white males in the system (Rasche, 1974). The impact of these educational developments on black inmates must be understood as limited by the racial segregation which existed in many prisons until quite recently. In 1968, the Unites States Supreme Court held that "segregation of the races in prisons and jails" is unconstitutional (*Lee* v. *Washington*, 1968) affirming the decision of a three-judge court, two years earlier, that Alabama statutes requiring racial segregation were a violation of the Fourteenth Amendment. In Alabama and other jurisdictions, segregation affected all aspects of inmate life: housing, classification, work assignments, dining facilities, recreation, appearance, discipline, and privileges.

When the courts described discrimination in work assignments, they referred to the noticeable concentration of blacks in low paying jobs. At Attica in 1971, the investigation revealed that there was racial discrimination in job assignments. It was found that white inmates held more than half of the jobs in the majority of the highly desirable job categories, even though they were only about 37 percent of the total prison population. Black inmates constituted 54 percent of the prison population and they along with Spanish-speaking inmates comprised over 75 percent of the inmates in the metal shop and the grading companies— both regarded as undesirable jobs (Attica, 1972). So far, specific references to racial discrimination in education have not been uncovered, but it is likely that access to education followed the pattern established for other aspects of incarceration.

Although the exact date of the Bureau's integration order is unknown, racial segregation in the federal prisons, described during its existence as giving "white and Negro prisoners equal opportunities and treatment without mixing them" (U.S. Department of Justice, 1943), ended some time before the Supreme Court's final denouement. Consequently, the following discussion of the current situation assumes integration to be real and enforceable in the federal prison system, in spite of cynicism about de facto segregation.

Overview of Education in the Federal Prison System

The Bureau of Prisons estimates that approximately 8,000 inmates are participating daily in some aspect of its educational program which is designed to provide "functional literacy, high school equivalency, marketable work skills, continuing education, personal growth experiences, and positive use of leisure time" (U.S. Department of Justice, 1976b). Toward that end, four components comprise the core of the education offerings: academic, occupational, social, and recreational. While each federal prison may offer each component, the programs may differ in depth and scope.

Essentially, the academic component deals with the intellectual sphere, ranging from basic skills courses for literacy, to bilingual competence and post-secondary work in the outside community. More specifically, academic education is comprised of Adult Basic Education (ABE), designed to bring the user to a sixth-grade reading, math, and writing level; Adult Secondary Education (ASE), designed to enable the user to complete a high school degree, usually through the General Equivalency Diploma (GED) test; post-secondary education (PSE), which provides courses for high school graduates, and is sometimes linked with degree possibilities such as the Associate of Arts (AA) degree; study release, which is essentially day parole, permits some inmates to attend local educational institutions. The Bureau claims that during 1975, about 9,000 inmates completed 9,000 college courses; 158 inmates obtained AA degrees; nineteen obtained bachelor's degrees; and two earned master's degrees (U.S. Department of Justice, 1975-76). Everything is taught in the prison, but post-secondary courses may also occur at the local community college or trade school. In this area, the greatest variety among institutional offerings is that which depends on outside linkages.

The basis of the occupational component is trade-employment experiences. The range of offerings at federal prisons includes those which are certified by an accrediting agency, such as Tool and Die Machinist at Lewisburg (Pa.), those which fulfill primarily institutional needs such as cooks at Milan (Mich.), and those which meet systemic needs such as the Federal Prison Industries data processing-keypunch shop at Alderson (W.Va.). These functions may converge on one trade, such as the printing of Bureau publications at the Prison Industries printing plant in Marion (Ill.), which is also an accredited apprenticeship

program in this field. The variety of occupational offerings among institutions
affects not only the inmate's skill development, but also his/her earnings during
incarceration, since "wages" vary. A welder can make up to $25 a month, while
a kitchen aide's limit is $10. The Prison Industries pay scale is higher. Conse-
quently, an inmate's occupation preferences may be determined by many factors:
income, outside job possibilities, parole board evaluation, ease or difficulty of
task, personal interest, and job status.

Social education and recreation are group counterparts to the individually
oriented academic and vocational components. These courses are noncredit and
may alter each semester. Social education can include lectures, films, workshops,
discussion groups led by inmates, staff, or community volunteers on such topics
as black culture, Indian studies, Spanish culture, theater, creative writing, yoga,
transactional analysis, Toastmasters, mood control, change agent, and conversa-
tional Spanish. Recreation is physical fitness and sports.

Until recently an inmate's ability to obtain a course depended on the priority of such an activity among other needs of that inmate, as determined by the
classification team, in consultation with the inmate. In the summer of 1976, the
Bureau decided that its retreat from the rehabilitation model meant that need
would no longer be a factor, and therefore participation would be voluntary
(U.S. Department of Justice, 1976b). The impact of this change in terms of inmate choices versus team recommendations remains to be seen.

One factor in the team's decision was the inmate's educational preparation,
as indicated by standardized test scores and formal schooling. Most inmates in
federal prisons have more than an eighth grade education and are in the average
range of intelligence. An examination of Table 11-2 reveals that blacks who have
gotten beyond the eighth grade (78 percent) slightly outnumber the others (70
percent), although the black inmates peaked just before finishing high school
while the others did not. Slightly over one-third of the blacks had completed
high school. Furthermore, black inmates seem to have taken greater advantage
of their intellectual potential to obtain an education than their contemporaries.
On I.Q. tests, blacks congregate in the middle range, while other inmates dom-
inate equally the average and above average ranges (arguments about the validity
of these tests notwithstanding). However, the percentage of average and above
average scoring blacks (78 percent) is exactly the same as the percentage of
blacks with some high school education (grades 9-12). The potential of other
inmates as indicated by their average and above average scores (92 percent) is
substantially greater than that group's high school educated students (70 percent).

Additional examination of the data showed that black women are generally
better educated than black men, but the men have higher I.Q. scores. That is,
more women have completed the formal schooling at every grade level but the
twelfth. However, more women score in the low I.Q. range, while men domi-
nate the average and above-average ranges. During imprisonment, women out-
numbered the men students (U.S. Department of Justice, 1975-76).

Table 11-2
Educational Preparation of Inmates in the Federal Prisons, 1976
(Percentages)

	All Inmates	*Black Inmates*	*Non-Black Inmates*
Highest Grade Completed			
0 to 5th grade	8	4	10
6th to 8th grade	19	18	20
9th to 11th grade	33	43	27
12th grade	40	35	43
I.Q. Scores			
Low scores (90 and below)	13	22	8
Average scores (91 to 110)	50	60	44
High scores (111 and above)	37	18	48

Source: U.S. Department of Justice, Bureau of Prisons. Computer Printout, Oct. 12, 1976.

Finally, a look at federal prison education from the input perspective—educational staff. The full-time professional education staff numbered 446. Of this number, 12.5 percent were black persons. An examination of the geographic distribution of black staff and black inmates shows that the greatest congruence occurs in the west, which has the fewest black inmates. The greatest difference occurs in the northeast, which has the most black inmates (Table 11-3). Nationally, there is approximately one education person for every fifty-seven inmates, and one black educator for every 163 black inmates.

Table 11-3
Regional Distribution of Black Inmates and Black Education Staff in the Federal Prisons, 1976

Region	*Inmates (Percent)*	*Education Staff (Percent)*
Northeast	56	12
Southeast	41	17
North-Central	37	7
South-Central	24	14
West	19	15

Source: U.S. Department of Justice, Bureau of Prisons, Education Branch. "Professional Education Staff, Women and Minorities, Aug. 31, 1976." Memo to Education Branch Administration, Oct. 12, 1976.

Co-Education at Fort Worth, Lexington, and Terminal Island

Since women have so consistently been ignored, even to the point of being denied programs and services available to men (Rasche, 1974), the institutions selected for investigation were those educating adult men and women simultaneously. This is possible because these institutions house men and women concurrently. The descriptive nomenclature is co-corrections.

Co-corrections in the federal system is a development of the past five years. It emphasizes programs and community contacts, rather than custody or industry and geographic isolation, in a minimum-medium security setting which does not segregate the sexes. Theoretically, men and women have equal and simultaneous access and use of all programs and facilities other than living and hospital arrangements. The concept is analogous to the co-educational college model. However, these are not educational institutions. As at all prisons, inmates recognize the power of systemwide and institution-specific regulations upon their lives. For example, sexual interaction other than hand-holding is punishable by transfer to another prison. Indeed, the threat of transfer from these comparatively open institutions provides considerable clout.

Co-corrections in the federal prisons was begun in late 1971, partly as an economic measure to deal with the high cost of incarcerating relatively small numbers of women. Since then, three opened, one closed, and one is in transition. At present, there are two such adult facilities: Fort Worth (Tex.), opened 1971, and Lexington (Ky.), opened 1974. Terminal Island (Calif.), opened a separate women's division in 1955 and is currently integrating some departments, such as education. Although Terminal Island is not actually co-correctional, the fact that it does provide co-education warranted its inclusion in this section.

Together these three prisons contained 8.5 percent of the federal prison population on June 30, 1976. On the same day, black inmates constituted 22 percent of the population at Terminal Island, 25 percent of Fort Worth, and 47 percent of Lexington (Table 11-4).

Table 11-4
Black Inmates in Federal Adult Co-Educational Institutions, 1976
(Percentages)

	Terminal Island (N = 888)		Fort Worth (N = 511)		Lexington (N = 750)	
	Men	Women	Men	Women	Men	Women
Black Inmates	22	30	17	44	40	60
Non-Black Inmates	78	70	83	56	60	40

Source: U.S. Department of Justice, Bureau of Prisons. "Population by Race." *Population Profiles Excluding Detentioners on June 30, 1976.* Computer Printout, 1976.

Each institution has a higher percentage of black women than black men. This is because there are fewer women's institutions, which congregates the women more than the men. The proportion of blacks is most in the eastern prison. This reflects somewhat the dispersion of blacks in the United States, and inmates are assigned in part on the basis of where they will live. Educational preparation data showed that the black inmates at Terminal Island had completed more schooling and scored somewhat higher on the I.Q. tests than those at Lexington and Fort Worth. Black inmates at all three institutions were somewhat better educated than others in the system; a greater percentage had completed nine to twelve years of formal education than did the aggregates (Table 11-5).

All these institutions provide considerable variety for each educational component (Appendixes 11A and 11B). Collectively and individually these three institutions provide occupational training in many areas that can be translated into employment outside of prison. They also list courses that are highly applicable to more personal aspects of living, such as transactional analysis, feminine development, and marriage and the family. In addition, classes pertaining to specific cultures and background are offered. Both Terminal Island and Lexington have as part of their curriculum classes related to the black experience. Fort Worth and Terminal Island have courses pertaining to Spanish culture. Overall, Forth Worth and Lexington offer a greater variety of courses than does Terminal Island. Similarly, Fort Worth and Lexington each have more than double the occupational enrollment of Terminal Island. In spite of the

Table 11-5
Educational Preparation of Black Inmates in Federal Adult Co-Educational Institutions, 1976
(Percentages)

	Terminal Island	Fort Worth	Lexington	All Black Inmates
Highest Grade Completed				
0 to 5th grade	2	1	3	4
6th to 8th grade	11	15	14	18
9th to 11th grade	40	49	49	43
12th grade	47	35	34	35
I.Q. Scores				
Low scores (90 and below)	14	35	28	22
Average scores (91 to 110)	62	61	58	60
High scores (111 and above)	24	4	13	18

Source: U.S. Department of Justice, Bureau of Prisons. Computer Printout, Oct. 12, 1976.

emphasis on community contacts, none had more than about 1 percent of the
inmates out on work release, and Terminal Island had the highest percentage.
Furthermore, only at Lexington were the few who did go equally male and
female; otherwise, it was man's work. Inasmuch as work release inmates are
paid the same rates as their outside coworkers, which is far in excess of inside
jobs, this area bears further investigation.

Participation in the academic component is greater than for the occupational,
except at Fort Worth, as Table 11-6 indicates. The larger academic group may
be a spillover from the considerable staff pressure for inmates to achieve a sixth-
grade competency (ABE). In comparing the potential students with the actual
enrolled ones, it is only at this level that the participation is overwhelming.
That is, at each institution the number of persons signed up for the ABE exceeds
those who have not completed sixth grade and are the program's targets. No
doubt there are many whose formal schooling goes beyond sixth grade but who
want/need math, reading, and bilingual work. However, this interest or pressure
does not persist to the next level, the high school degree (ASE). Less than 15
percent of all inmates are enrolled in the adult secondary education program,
although between 45 percent and 60 percent claimed they had not completed
twelfth grade (U.S. Department of Justice, 1975-76).

Finally, a comment about budget and staff at the local level. While it is
commonly believed that more money and more staff would mean more students,
it is not so in the prison context. Among the three institutions described, Lexington has the smallest budget and staff and the same or larger enrollment
(Table 11-7). The enrollment was dominated by Lexington not only in the
aggregate, but at almost every level. How this came to be so is not clear.

These three co-educational institutions certainly provide models for education in correctional settings. This investigation did not evaluate the quality of
the instruction nor requirements for enrollment in the courses. However, the
variety of courses and programs offered seem to at least indicate an attempt to
provide inmates with marketable skills and personal growth experiences.

Table 11-6
Academic and Occupational Enrollments, 1975-76
(Percentages)

	Academic Students	Occupational Students
Terminal Island	28	11.5
Fort Worth	19	23.1
Lexington	29	23.4

Source: U.S. Department of Justice, Bureau of Prisons, Correctional
Programs Division, Programs Reporting Systems Branch. *Raps II
Reports.* Washington, D.C.: Bureau of Prisons, Oct. 1975 - June 1976.

Table 11-7
Budget and Staff Among the Federal Co-Educational
Institutions, 1976

	Education Budget	*Education Staff*
Terminal Island	$267,000 (8%)	One to every 23 inmates ($N = 32$)
Fort Worth	$343,000 (8.4%)	One to every 17 inmates ($N = 24$)
Lexington	$307,000 (4%)	One to every 49 inmates ($N = 14$)

Source: U.S. Department of Justice, Bureau of Prisons, Budget Office. "Consolidated Obligations and Per Capita Cost, FY76." Mimeo, 1976.

Conclusions

This cursory investigation of correctional education at three federal facilities has revealed that relevant educational programs can be a reality in prisons. It further demonstrates that diverse offerings can be available. Inmates can acquire the basic academic tools, such as reading and arithmetic, and can even progress to higher levels of academic excellence, including high school and college degrees. Further opportunities at becoming proficient at a trade or in a skill area can also be a part of the total curriculum. Programs and courses that are geared towards personal growth and improvement are also realistic possibilities in the prison setting.

However, the techniques for constructing good academic and educational programs and courses has never been a problem—either in prison or out of prison. The problem has been how students are selected for the existing programs, what criteria are used, and who selects the students. The failure of educational institutions in providing quality education and relevant education for all segments of society has been well documented.

For all inmates, and especially blacks, education is crucial. Therefore, education in prison deserves the same scrutiny it gets on the outside. Questions must be asked. What is available and who may obtain it? What does the content indicate about the purposes? What does support for funding and staff indicate about commitment to a program, to its students? Why is it that the Lexington facility which has the highest percentage of black inmates has the lowest percentage of its total budget allocated to education and the lowest staff-inmate ratio? Given all the controversy surrounding the use of intelligence tests, especially with minority populations, how is testing used and justified in correctional education programs? Are students selected for programs based on the I.Q. scores? What implications can be drawn from a low black staff-black inmate ratio? Are the educational interests of the inmates, the staff, the officials in congruence or in conflict?

This investigation revealed that only slightly over one-third of the black inmates completed high school. This means that at the beginning, most black inmates will be concerned with academic courses and programs of a noncollege nature (ABE, ASE). Who teaches the courses, the content, and the teacher-student ratio are especially sensitive areas. In addition, the occupational curriculum will be of paramount importance. Policies and issues such as who goes on work release, how much financial aid is available, union restrictions, and what are realistic occupational training experiences will affect black inmates.

Finally, this examination of education in the federal prisons, and Fort Worth, Lexington, and Terminal Island in particular, was not intended to ignore the reality that most prisoners have much less. Indeed, it was intended to emphasize that inmates at other institutions *cannot* have it better, only varying degrees of worse.

Most institutions do not have the variety offered at the coed prisons, nor would program participation be as high a priority. Education cannot yet compete with prison industries, institutional maintenance, group counseling, and other demands on available institution program time. Therefore, students go to school in the evening, the only hours set aside for education; space for study and privacy is limited; library facilities and access time are inadequate (McCollum, 1976). Inmate students who want a college education may have to work all day to finance the night class or correspondence course. Their income is limited by the types of jobs which exist at that prison and their ability to affect institutional mores regarding assignments. Federal prisoners are also handicapped by rules which require they pay the higher out-of-state tuition rates because they are not recognized as residents of the state in which they are incarcerated. Consequently, institutional transfers, which are rarely education motivated, can really be costly. Not only is the tuition nonrefundable, but the credits may not be transferable. This also affects the vocational student, who may not be able to complete a particular training program, such as dental technician, begun at one prison but non-existent at the other.

What happens to people while they do time in prison may, or may not, directly affect what happens to them afterwards. Regardless of the skills which may be acquired, inmates are always subject to the value-laden socialization of their institution, a process intended to change the inmates and their post-prison behavior. Education continues to be an important change agent, and thus bears watching.

Prisons are filled with uneducated people, evidence of the failings of American public schools. The population that has been victimized by an inadequate education has by and large been the population that now populates our juvenile institutions and adult prisons. Correctional educators must adopt the strengths and creativity of education outside prison. There aren't many options left if they fail.

References

Attica: The Official Report of the New York State Special Commission on Attica. New York: Praeger Publishers, 1972.

Dell'Apa, Frank. *Education Programs in Adult Correctional Institutions: A survey.* Bolder, Colo.: Western Interstate Commission for Higher Education, 1973.

Lee v. Washington, 88 S. CT. 994,390; U.S. 333,334, 1968.

Lekkerkerker, Eugenia. *Reformatories for Women in the United States.* The Hague, Holland: J.B. Wolters, 1931.

MacCormack, Austin H. *The Education of Adult Prisoners.* New York: National Society for Penal Information, 1926, 1931.

McCollum, Sylvia G. "New Designs for Correctional Education and Training Programs." *Federal Probation,* June 1973, pp. 6-11.

Michael, Calvin B. "Changing Inmates Through Education." In *Education and Training in Correctional Institutions: Proceedings of a Conference.* University of Wisconsin: Center for Studies in Vocational and Technical Education, 1968, pp. 95-105.

National Committee on Prisons and Prison Labor, Committee on the Care and Training of Delinquent Women and Girls. *Industries for Correctional Institutions for Women: Survey Report.* New York: National Committee on Prisons and Prison Labor, 1927.

Rasche, Christine. "The Female Offender as an Object of Criminological Research." In A.M. Brodsky (ed.), *The Female Offender.* Special issue of *Criminal Justice and Behavior* 1 (1974):301-320.

Roberts, Alton R. *Sourcebook on Prison Education.* Springfield, Ill.: Charles C. Thomas, 1971.

U.S. Department of Justice, Bureau of Prisons. *Annual Report 1943.* Washington, D.C.: Government Printing Office, 1943.

U.S. Department of Justice, Bureau of Prisons, Education Branch. *Adult Education in Corrections,* prepared by Sylvia G. McCollum. Draft copy, 1976a, pp. 41-42.

U.S. Department of Justice, Bureau of Prisons. *Education for Tomorrow.* Washington, D.C.: Bureau of Prisons, 1976b.

U.S. Department of Justice, Bureau of Prisons. *Population Profiles Excluding Detentioners on June 30, 1976.* Computer printout, 1976c.

U.S. Department of Justice, Bureau of Prisons, Correctional Program Division, Programs Reporting Systems Branch. *Raps II Reports.* Washington, D.C.: Bureau of Prisons, Oct. 1975-June 1976.

Appendix 11A

Federal Bureau of Prisons Social
Education Offerings by Institution

Course of Study	Terminal Island	Fort Worth	Lexington
Black Studies/Culture	x		x
Change Agent		x	
Chicano Culture		x	
Coping Skills		x	
Creative Writing	x		x
Dale Carnegie	x		
Debate	x		
Feminine Development		x	x
Guides for Better Living		x	
Human Relations	x		
Indian Studies	x		
Journalism		x	x
Marriage and the Family		x	
Mexican-American Studies	x		
Money Management	x		
Motivational Classes		x	
Positive Mental Attitudes			x
Spanish Culture/Conversation		x	x
Transactional Analysis		x	

Source: U.S. Department of Justice, Bureau of Prisons, *Education for Tomorrow*, (Washington, D.C.: Government Printing Office), 1976, pp. 18-24.

Appendix 11B

Federal Bureau of Prisons Occupational Education Offerings by Institution

Course of Study	Terminal Island	Fort Worth	Lexington
Auto Tune-Up*			x
Barbering*			x
Basic Hematology			x
Blueprint Reading		x	
Building Maintenance		x	
Business Education	x		
Business Machine Repairs			x
Career Guidance/Development		x	x
Child Development		x	
Cosmetology			x
Drafting	x	x	
Drapery Manufacturing			x
Electronics		x	
Food Service	x	x	
Gourmet Cooking			x
Home Economics	x		
Hospital Attendant			x
Ironworker		x	
Keypunch	x	x	
Meatcutting			x
Nursing Assistant			x
Printing		x	
Secretary II		x	
TV Production		x	
Typing		x	
Welding	x		x
X-Ray Technician			x

*On the job training.

Source: U.S. Department of Justice, Bureau of Prisons, *Education for Tomorrow* (Washington, D.C.: Government Printing Office), 1976, pp. 18-24.

12

Higher Education: Roles in Criminal Justice

Jimmy Bell

Traditionally, when American society has experienced a serious social problem or has been confronted by danger of some kind, higher education has responded by lending research experience and expertise to the search for solutions (Newman, 1975). Major societal concerns including illness, poverty, overpopulation, and space exploration have been perceived as mandates for action by professional researchers; colleges and universities have trained and recruited appropriate manpower.

Crime in this country is viewed by many as the nation's foremost social problem, requiring that the first priority should be an effort toward reducing criminal activities. This problem is not new, but the successful implementation of a merger with higher education is significantly lacking in substance. One must ask if crime is viewed by postsecondary education as a concern of the same serious magnitude as the previously mentioned social problems.

The Roles of Higher Education

Crime has reached alarming proportions in the black communities (Parker and Brownfield, 1974; U.S. Department of Justice, 1975). In fact, it is so serious that society must ask how the criminal justice system can minimize and reduce this excessive criminal behavior in the black community. The answer, in part, rests with responsible practitioners and academicians who must pool their technical and scholarly resources to meet this challenge.

Viable research with strong social implications regarding the nature of confinement and reintegration to the community is essential. Colleges and universities can provide this valuable effort.

Training sensitive and responsible personnel for the justice system is another area for significant contributions by higher education. Since blacks have consistently been underrepresented as personnel in the system (Chrisman, 1971; Crockett, 1972; Egerton, 1974), post-secondary institutions need to actively recruit blacks into their programs for law, criminal justice, and/or correctional psychology. Where such programs are not easily available, institutions of higher learning must develop them.

Additional involvement of higher education should include educational opportunities for those incarcerated. Qualified inmates should be encouraged to participate in post-secondary programs that embrace the notion of

113

self-expression, value clarification, and alternatives to criminal behavior. This area of rich potential has been discussed earlier in the book (Chapter 11).

Finally, higher education can contribute toward solving the problem of crime in the black community by becoming directly involved, both in the community and in the criminal justice system. This service function is as valuable as all other vehicles for joining higher education and criminal justice.

Research and Criminal Justice

Social disorders occurring both inside and outside prisons have enormous social implications for blacks and others involved with criminal justice, both as offenders and as personnel. Research should seek to explain and illuminate factors that lead to black crime and confinement. Available data suggest that incarceration in this country is disproportionately reserved for blacks and people of low economic status. Are there attributes of America's correctional system which magnetize the poor, blacks, and other minorities in this country? Research can guide efforts to understand and rehabilitate black criminals, to understand and help black victims, to understand and increase the number of competent black personnel, and to understand and eliminate inequitable justice.

To merely engage in criminal justice research about blacks is not enough. Colleges and universities must also raise research questions. What research is likely to produce data which will suggest remedial approaches? What is the nature of the questions asked? What purpose is the research effort to serve? From what vantage point is the problem being viewed? Whom does the problem affect?

Answers to these questions and many more should carefully guide the researcher who seeks to improve the present system in America. These questions have significance because much research in corrections and other components of the criminal justice system has been "agency determined" and subordinated to various institutional interests (Blumer, 1967). Formulation of research problems by institutions of higher learning, particularly by blacks trained in various aspects of criminal justice, may avoid the biases within the criminal justice system.

To retain objectivity is, however, difficult. According to Anthony Platt (1971), many private foundations have poured millions of dollars into carefully specified action research in various criminal justice centers throughout the country. Government-sponsored research is another example of special interest research. Platt further states that the rise of the "multiversity" in recent years as a "broker" between scholars and funding agencies has served to strengthen and institutionalize relationships. Scholars have been encouraged to formulate research which is politically acceptable to established agencies. Platt also maintains that the research marketplace, dominated by large foundations and the government, is structured in such a way that research grants, prestige, facilities, and other fringe benefits are more easily achieved by scholars who are willing to work on behalf of the state and its official institutions. Perhaps this accounts for the negative portrayal of blacks in research on criminal justice, as discussed in Chapter 4.

This kind of research is detrimental to society in general and it tends to retard the very criminal justice system it purports to aid and improve. Fortunately, a great deal of scholarly research is not determined by agency mandates. Higher education institutions can promote the scholarly responsibility and accountability which is still the predominating source of scientific inquiry.

Criminal Justice Education

Many criminal justice administrators acknowledge, some more than others, that the field is in need of personnel with more knowledge, expertise, integrity, and initiative. This should not be viewed as an indictment against criminal justice practitioners; rather, it is a commendation to correctional administrators who may have identified a particular problem in a specific area that needs attention. Criminal justice must utilize the available services which universities offer in order to resolve the conflict of their unmanifested destiny. Today's inequitable criminal justice processes and philosophy will not suffice for tomorrow's correctional realities.

The university should serve as a broker of integrity between the criminal justice system and the community. To impact the black experience, universities should attempt to determine what the needs are in correctional institutions and design appropriate action. In-service training programs offered through the university may prove to be invaluable. Programs developed within correctional institutional settings are believed to be equally rewarding.

University professors could encourage their students to establish a voluntary inmate correspondence program to facilitate communication with the "free community" and the "inmate community." Obviously there are many advantages in this type of arrangement. There is reciprocal information sharing between the parties involved that may prove mutually rewarding. For the student aspiring to a career in correctional counseling much could be learned about the "inside world" of the inmate. On the other hand, the sessions may be therapeutic for the inmate, whose anxieties may be relieved to some degree just by knowing that someone cares.

Involving Higher Education for Action

Universities can become actively involved within the criminal justice system itself. Every university should organize a corrections committee to function with the state department of corrections. This committee must become actively involved with criminal justice affairs of the state and the local community.

Educators and correctional practitioners could establish a standardized inmate classification system, such as discussed in Chapter 14. This system, unlike current methods in corrections, should adopt a behavioral approach, which asserts that individuals develop a basic set of tendencies, needs, and capacities as a result of social interaction. The range of behavioral characteristics surely must not be so nearly infinite that it defies categorization. Indeed, many criminologists suggest that man commits crime either out of "greed" or "need." This dichotomy, though simplistic, warrants further investigation. The behavioral approach emphasizes treatment as opposed to the more traditional punishment approach currently anchored in the American philosophy of corrections.

Surveys could be made within the institutions to determine the marketable skills of black inmates. Subsequently, surveys could be made in communities regarding the need for these skills. This procedure has implications for prerelease, work release, parole, diversification, therapy, and special services to list a few.

Conclusion

It is unarguable that blacks and other minorities constitute a vast disproportion of individuals held captive in America's confinement systems. It is equally undebatable that non-blacks disproportionately manage these same confinement systems. It is almost as if correctional practitioners are daring any segment of the population to challenge its credibility. The result is constant conflict.

In order for academicians and correctional administrators to link efforts to reduce crime and its particular impact on the black community, the parties involved must come together to discuss common goals, objectives, and interests. Research, in part, must be designed to assist criminal justice to achieve its ultimate goals, assuming that these goals do not conflict with the academicians' professional and scientific values. Conversely, correctional administrators must be cooperative and willing to engage in planned activities that are designed to be mutually rewarding for the entire society. Through a continuous cycle of planning, implementing, and evaluating, the merger of education and corrections can be successfully realized.

References

Blumer, Herbert. *Threats From Agency-Determined Research: The Case of Camelot.* Cambridge, Mass.: Massachusetts Institute of Technology Press, 1967.

Chrisman, Robert. "Black Prisoners, White Law." *The Black Scholar.* April-May 1971, pp. 44-46.

Crockett, George W. Jr. "Commentary: Black Judges and the Black Judicial Experience." *Wayne Law Review,* Nov. 1972, pp. 61-71.

Egerton, John. "Minority Police: How Many Are There?" *Race Relations Reporter,* Nov. 1974, pp. 19-21.

Newman, Donald J. *Introduction to Criminal Justice.* Philadelphia: J.B. Lippincott, 1975.

Parker, J.A. and Allen G. Brownfield. *What the Negro Can Do About Crime.* New York: Arlington House Publishers, 1974.

Platt, Anthony. *Politics of Riot Commissions.* New York: MacMillan Publishers, 1971.

U.S. Department of Justice, Law Enforcement Assistance Administration. *Criminal Victimization in the United States 1973,* Advance Report. Washington, D.C.: Government Printing Office, 1975.

13 Improving Police Relations in the Black Community

L. Alex Swan

Introduction

In spite of the increased concern for better police-community relations, and the great number of police-community programs, the relationship which still exists between the police and the black community is anomalous, parasitical, and suspicious. The police are viewed, perhaps even more than before, as an outside force which continually invades and occupies the community. This situation persists in many respects because of both the law enforcement officers' and the community members' perception of the inability of the community to satis-factorily neutralize and eliminate the oppressive nature of the police function.

Many of the current programs related to police-community relations direct efforts and strategies toward changing the attitudes, perceptions, and ultimately the behavior of the policeman. There is no doubt that this goal is desirable and should be achieved; nonetheless, there are no convincing data that this goal has yet been achieved. Many of these programs either explicitly or implicitly view the black community as a powerless entity which, therefore, lessens the com-munity's ability to demand accountability. Police-community relations, by and large, are not designed to enhance the capability of the community to construc-tively solve its own police-community problems.

What seems lacking in many black communities is a structure which will insure, by its own operation and in conjunction with other programs designed to reduce crime and protect the community members, that police behavior will be accountable and responsive to the community. Any structure adopted to fill this vacuum for the community should be based on the assumption that not only does the community need protection from those individuals who commit crimes against the community, but it needs protection from those individuals who are officially defined as its protectors, who also commit crimes against the com-munity. Simply controlling crime committed by members of the community will not guarantee residents protection from law enforcement officers. Much of the police oppression and brutality in the fifties and sixties had very little to do with crime control. What mechanism can be implemented that can change the oppressive and negative definitions held by the police of the community and which are operationalized by behaviors at the community level?

Adapted, with permission, from L. Alex Swan, "Crime Prevention and the Protection of Lives: A Mechanism to Change Police Behavior in the Community," *Journal of Afro-American Issues* (May 1974): 119-128.

Status of the Black Community

Before this question is addressed, an analysis of the status of the black community and its relationship to the larger society must be evaluated. The American
society has historically been structured economically, politically, and socially in
a way that the black community has encountered severe employment and educational discrimination, political domination, economic exploitation and excessive legal constraints. In this context, the status of the black community in the
American society can be equated to that of a colony. Tabb (1970), in his review
of the status of the black ghetto, suggests that a colonial relationship exists
where there is (1) economic control and exploitation and (2) political dependence
and subjugation; both of these conditions necessitate separation and an inferior
status. Geographically, politically, and economically the black community reflects this colonized status. The political and economic decisions and policies
made in America tend to assign the black community to a politically and economically powerless position in relation to political and economic institutions
external to the community. The means of production are generally not resident
in the community and neither are they owned by members of the black community. Moreover, the mode of production is designed for the well-being and
economic success of the few at the expense of the masses. Therefore, the circu-
lar flow of monies in our society is such that it stabilizes power economically,
and without this economic base any use of political power by the black community is ineffective. Even with some degree of political control of the community at the local level by community members, the economic relationship
which has forced an extralegal political subservience upon the black community
and its members will continue to exist.

   The colonized relationship of black communities is an integral and necessary
part of the institutional structure of the American society. In order to maintain
this relationship, the black community is made a focal point for the administration and oppressive control by policemen who also seek legitimation by the
black community. In this framework, one very real concern of the black community residents should be what the community can do for the police and itself
rather than what the policemen can do for the community. Any mechanism to
correct some of the defects, overcome deficiencies, broaden perspectives, ask
new questions, and provide new answers must offer new paradigms to enhance
the power of the community to protect itself.

Opinions and Coping Behavior of Community Members

In the black community, like other communities, residents form patterns of
informal and formal interaction with each other to solve personal and community problems. Such forms of interaction in the black community, however,

usually seem to be related to specific events such as emergency situations which are difficult to resolve without a united community effort. For a variety of reasons these types of group interactions are usually not sustained for long periods of time nor do they generally include a large percentage of the community residents. This is not to suggest that the community members who are not participants are not as concerned about change as those who are involved. Those residents not actively participating in formal community gatherings may not agree on the methods utilized for resolving community problems or they may feel a sense of community powerlessness but may still share the same goals and objectives as those that are involved.

Contrary to the opinions of many who view the black community in a negative light, there are many community members very much concerned about the high rate of crime in their community. In both an absolute and a relative sense, community members believe that major and minor crimes occur in their community with alarming regularity.

Those who commit major or minor crimes in the black community are usually familiar with the community and its members, and attempt to maximize the fear of the community by taking advantage of the powerlessness and immobility of the community members. These perpetrators of crimes in the community are usually young men of the community or of an adjoining community. Whether the lawbreakers are external to the community or a part of the community, the majority of community members want both the major and minor crimes reduced and eliminated.

Communities that lack the power to control crime in their areas use alternative patterns of coping with crime. Noninvolvement is one way of coping with the danger members sense in the community and is probably the technique that is used most. This is the case, for the most part, because members of the community are afraid for their lives and property. More importantly, they sense that they are not really protected from danger by the police, except in some instances in an after-the-fact fashion. If these members—the seemingly unconcerned and noninvolved—believed that they were protected from real or imagined danger, they could possibly be stimulated to become involved and might contribute to a decrease in the crime rate.

A significant number of community members are victims of crimes. This vulnerability to criminal acts in conjunction with after-the-fact nature of the police function, prompt community residents to take prudent steps to avoid being victimized. The precautions taken include avoiding groups of teenagers, locking car doors, installing extra door locks, limiting activities after dark, avoiding being alone on the street after dark, and avoiding the police who are supposed to be their protection. In some respects, these actions to deal with the threat of crime and unfair treatment by police disrupt the free flowing lives of the community members. These protective measures are not necessarily drastic, but their use tends to reduce the fear of crime and the possibility of being victimized and brutalized by police and/or community members.

There was a time when residents were not particularly reluctant to intervene when they could assist others who were being victimized. Today, community members may hear victims crying for help, or even see an attempt being made to commit a crime, and not intervene. This attitudinal change from concern and involvement to uninvolvement causes alienation among residents and heightens the fear of crime in individuals in the community.

The nature of the community's problem is perceived in similar ways by the police and community members. However, the etiology of such problems, for the police, is internal in the community and has racial overtones. The community members, locating the cause as being both external and internal to the community, believe crime persists because the police either choose not to do or are incapable of doing anything about it in terms of consistent control and prevention.

There are three broad categories in which black community members generally place the causes of crime: (1) inadequate or inappropriate family socialization including poor home environments, illegitimacy, inconsistency or lack of discipline and parental control; (2) the economic factors of poverty resulting from underemployment or unemployment; and (3) political and economic oppression of black communities by the external white community.

Those who view poverty and childrearing practices as the causes of crime advocate crime prevention programs centering on employment, recreation, and other community action programs for the youth. These programs as vehicles for crime prevention are important and should be operationalized by community members at the community level. However, while these programs can address concerns about unemployment and childrearing practices, they are only part of the answer. The fact is that individuals who are known to have been financially solvent have been convicted of crimes such as those which exist in their community. Moreover, there are many people who are poor and who are not criminal. There are also children who have grown up in homes where poor childrearing practices existed and who did not become criminals and, conversely, children reared in homes considered by all standards to be good home environments who were later labeled as criminal.

Those who conceptualize crime in terms of oppression relate the reduction of crime in the black community to political and economic independence and control of the community by its members. In those communities where the ethnic group can be free of external domination and have a high degree of community interest, responsibility, supervision, and control, crime rates will be lower. There is no doubt that community crime prevention programs are very much needed; however, ethnic and community control of the community and the agencies which operate within its boundaries is a very vital component which can enhance the possibility of the other programs operating efficiently to protect community members and reduce the incidence of crime.

Depending on the nature of their interactions with the police, community

members will articulate diverse opinions concerning the effectiveness of the
police's effort in the area of crime control. For the most part, the police will be
seen as ineffective if they do not work with community residents in a cooperative
venture to control crime. Community members deem this joint effort as crucial
to a successful effort. Any cooperative effort will be seriously hampered by those
police who merely verbalize a commitment to this cooperative thrust while concurrently blaming the community for not cooperating with them in fighting
crime.

Community relations programs have generally not brought desirable results
to the black community. Consequently, many community members still view
the police as being discourteous, brutal, partial, insulting, and irresponsible in
performing their duties. There are still those who place more value on the stolen
property in a robbery than on human life.

These reasons contribute to the lack of community support for the police.
In additon to a general ambivalence on the part of the community members
concerning the moral state of affairs in the police department, some residents
are convinced that the police are seldom present when they are really needed.
Moreover, they suspect that this is true in part because of the police perception
of the community and their traditionally irresponsible attitude toward black
people. These conditions must be corrected if community members are to sense
the feeling of protection that the presence of the police is supposed to inspire.

Some policemen attribute their inability to control crime as related to manpower, poor salaries, and limited police authority and power, while the community focuses on such factors as lack of understanding of black communities
and lack of proper police training as critical factors in the lack of crime control
in the community. What is suggested by some is that crime in the community
(narcotics, prostitution, etc.) is functional for many police and they would
hesitate to see it controlled, preferring to have crime continue in communities
which have little internal power. In this regard, many community members
sense that the level of protection they receive is limited and in some cases is
nonexistent. It is therefore not so much the presence or absence of the police
which explains the increase or decrease of crime rates, but rather the nature of
the presence of the police in the community and the power status in the community.

Any structure established to change the behavior of the police to insure
greater accountability to the black community must provide for protection to
the residents of the community and the prevention of the occurrences and con-
tinuance of crime. These functions should be complemented by a variety of
supportive services and programs.

Community Mechanism

The proposed community mechanism speaks to the demands of citizens for

greater participation in legally protecting their lives and property. It translates
goals and concerns for the reduction of crime, police brutality, and the protection of lives into action that seeks to reduce the problems faced by the police
and the community. The objective is to increase the internal control of the
community to the point that it is possible for these problems to be solved
promptly, effectively, and with a high degree of consistency.

Community control of the community and the community's institutions
and their services is an antecedent condition to the solution of many of the
problems now facing the community. Those who staunchly maintain that
better cooperative police-community relations is the solution see the police
taking the initiative for change. The available evidence does not indicate that
this initiative is forthcoming or that it embodies the necessary and sufficient
ingredients to accomplish this goal.

The structure should be such that it can help to maximize police-citizen
interaction to enhance courteous and respectful behavior toward community
members; increase knowledge and understanding of the events occurring in
the community; and encourage interaction with members of that community
which the police are serving. The mechanism should allow for easy recognition
of the areas of deficiencies in police training and provide for input into the
training program so that deficient areas can be corrected. More efficient identification and reporting of those police who are involved in illegal activities in
the community should occur as a result. Those police involved in gambling,
numbers, narcotics, payoffs, and other criminal activities and misconduct
should be dealt with through the community mechanism. It must guarantee
that the police behavior stay within the bounds of the law, and that the beat-
ings, false arrests, and harassment of citizens will cease. The mechanism should
provide for community recruitment for the police department.

The mechanism for change must also help to reduce the threatening or
the potentially threatening nature of the contacts between community residents
and the police. This applies to both the residents and policemen being fearful
for their lives. In addition, prompt responses of the police to the request for
service by residents must be assured. This can be achieved if the proximity
of the police to the community is such that it makes it easy for them to respond
quickly and there is a more personal relationship between the police patrolling
the neighborhood and the residents.

Many community members report that certain police behaviors are abrasive
to them. There should be an effective formal way to voice complaints about
police behavior that is not associated with a "downtown" concept of police
protection and services. Consequently, the mechanism must also have the
potential to effectively personalize and localize complaint procedures. Included
in the mechanism should be some procedure to decrease the probability of
accusing the police falsely. When the procedure works effectively, fair hearings
of complaints against the police will result in appropriate action.

Area Agency

The area agency is established to house the operations of the police. The first step in developing the mechanism is to increase community input into this agency. The following points define the general structure and function of an area police agency:

1. The area police agency should be physically located within the communities where the majority of black people live; it should be staffed by policemen who live within the community.

2. The area agency should have several facilitating components which would enhance positive police-community relations. Included in the area agencies should be social relations programs; communication programs; a process for resolving resident complaints; and police disciplinary procedures.

3. The community members should have an opportunity to receive and meet each policeman who works in the community at community meetings, and necessary information about the officer should be communicated to the community at such a meeting.

4. Refresher courses, seminars, and group sessions should be offered on a regular basis to keep the officers up-to-date on techniques and strategies of policing.

5. Each officer should submit a monthly report describing his/her crime prevention activities.

The area agency will be represented by an area agency policeperson on all of the larger police agency (downtown) internal committees with full voting power. This representative will make relevant and necessary presentations to these committees on behalf of the community. A formal feedback channel should be initiated from the downtown area through this representative.

Supervisory Board

The next step in developing the mechanism is to divide the community into districts of equal population and select a supervisory board to oversee the area agency. Representatives should be elected by the members of each district, and each community organization (NAACP, Urban League, SCLC, CORE, etc.) should have one representative. These district representatives, the organization representatives, and three representatives of the police will constitute the official community-police supervisory board. All members of the supervisory board must live in the district of which they are representatives.

The supervisory board may determine what kind of relationship the area agency will have with other institutions, organizations, and programs external and internal to the community and its members. The functional policies of the board are to be made by the supervisory board. The supervisory board will also concern itself with the following:

1. Interdepartmental area agency discipline, questionable activities and behavior of the police and other problems reported to the board through the area
agency. In order to adequately process and resolve police-community concerns,
the board may have to meet at least once a month.

2. Recruiting, interviewing, and final acceptance of a police officer to work
in the area agency, other area agencies, and the larger downtown agency.

3. Regular meetings with community organizations and the general community either in committee form or by mass meeting.

4. A system of communication to keep the public informed of the board's
activities and the police activities in the community.

Advisory Board

An advisory board whose main function will be to provide advice and counsel to
the supervisory board and the larger community concerning the operations of
area agencies will be established. Each area agency will have an advisory board
consisting of a representative from each district, a representative from the supervisory board, and a representative from the area agency. This board may meet
once per quarter or at any other time on the request of the supervisory board.
The advisory and supervisory boards must be directly responsible to their district, to the area agency, to community organizations, and to the general program for better police-community relations.

Conclusion

This structure provides for community resident input at all levels of police-
community relations. Residents not only have an opportunity to meet new
police people assigned to their jurisdiction, but they also have a vehicle for
selecting representatives to the various boards, and receiving feedback from
their representatives. Community residents would have real power to participate in setting policies, resolving disputes, employing and dismissing police,
establishing police-community relations programs, and increasing community
input and output on its own behalf. As a result, they can demand more
accountability from the police.

This community mechanism does not intend to dictate the day-to-day
operation, such as procedure for election, length of time to be served on
boards, the ideal size of districts, and other facets of the process. These are
best decided by each city, depending on its own unique characteristics.

In order to control and restrict crime in the black community, it is
necessary that the police force erase the negative image that has historically
been associated with its presence in the black community. Merely placing

"helpful" police in the black community is not the total answer. There must be some feeling of community and some sense of responsiveness and accountability to the community.

It is imperative that the black communities in America begin to feel the same sense of protection from the police force that other more affluent white communities feel. It is important that they become involved in controlling the forces that impinge on their lives and that they can have a voice in correcting some of the injustices that occur to them. This program, if implemented, can begin to meet the needs of the community relative to the protection of lives and property and the reduction of crime. Any reform or reorganization of the regular police department is only a small part of the solution and does not incisively address itself to the concerns of the black community. This mechanism is designed to reduce the distance between police and the community and provide real methods of handling police-community friction.

Reference

Tabb, William K. *The Political Economy of the Black Ghetto.* New York: W.W. Norton and Co., 1970.

14

Classifying Black Inmates: The Alabama Prison Classification Project

Charles E. Owens

In January 1976, the Alabama Board of Corrections was prohibited by federal Judge Frank Johnson from admitting any additional adult offenders to the already overcrowded state penal institutions. In the same year, the University of Alabama's Center for Correctional Psychology was given responsibility for the prison classification system. Their mission was to reclassify the approximately 4,000 adult inmates in the Alabama prison system. This undertaking became known as the Alabama Prison Classification Project (PCP). The following report provides my observations and interpretations of that project as a participant-observer.

Background

The circumstance that led to the classification project was provided by Mr. Worley James, an eighty-one-year-old black inmate who had spent approximately thirty years of his life in prison. In 1974, Mr. James sent a two-page handwritten habeas corpus to Judge Johnson in which he asserted that a number of constitutional violations had been perpetrated against him; among these was the right to rehabilitation. The writ was drafted by a nineteen-year-old black inmate serving a life sentence for robbery. The original writ, later consolidated with other suits (*James* v. *Wallace* and *Pugh* v. *Locke*, 1976), eventually proved the Alabama prison system to be guilty of violations of the Eighth Amendment (cruel and unusual punishment) and the Fourteenth Amendment (due process and equal protection).

It was shown through a pretrial investigation, expert testimony, and voluminous documents that conditions existed in the prisons which fostered unsanitary living and food service conditions. It was also found that there was no functional classification system used to identify various segments of the population, such as the aged and infirmed, the mentally retarded, the psychologically disturbed, and the illiterate who needed special services. Additionally, violent-aggressive inmates were not separated from nonviolent inmates; inmates did not have the opportunity to participate in vocational-educational program; and work release facilities and recreational opportunities were lacking.

The Alabama prison population affected by the court order was composed of approximately 61 percent black males and 75 percent black females (University of Alabama, 1974). The guards, however, have historically been white and from rural areas; the institutions have been located in rural settings.

In addition to the disproportionate incarceration of blacks, other discrepancies were noted. Out of a total of 135 executions in the state, 107 (79 percent) have been black. Twenty-two inmates have been executed for rape; twenty of these (90 percent) were black (U.S. Department of Justice, 1976). Black males have been incarcerated at a rate more than four times greater than that for white males (University of Alabama, 1974).

Black inmates have also made allegations about racial injustices and the racially oppressive atmosphere in the prisons. In fact, a daily attendance sign at one of the maximum security prisons designated the population as "white" or "colored." The term "colored" was converted to "black" in 1976. Another racial irregularity was the higher number of blacks in road camps. There were three times as many blacks as whites in road camps (University of Alabama, 1974). Racial tension surfaced in 1974 when a prison disturbance resulted in the deaths of two black inmates by guards, one black inmate by an alleged suicide, and one prison guard by inmates. In addition, nine other black inmates are being tried for the death of the guard ("Alabama," 1975). These nine black inmates became known as the now renown Atmore-Holman Brothers. So far, one Atmore-Holman Brother has been sentenced to die.

Classification

As a result of deficiencies within the prison system, the court mandated the establishment of a classification system to identify (1) inmates in need of specialized services (aged and infirmed, mentally retarded, illiterate, and psychologically disturbed); (2) inmates for whom transfer to a pre-release, work release, or community-based facility would be appropriate; and (3) the violent inmate in order to separate him from the nonviolent inmate. In addition, the PCP was to assist in assessing the inmates' needs and abilities for participation in a basic education program and/or a vocational training program.

A review of numerous classification plans in the American Correctional Association's *Correctional Classification and Treatment* (Hippchen, 1975) showed that most of the plans incorporated, in varying degrees, the use of the following techniques and/or procedures in arriving at classification decisions: testing, individual and team interviews with inmates, inmate records, institutional behavior, and medical examinations.

These also formed the basis for the Alabama Prison Classification Project. Each monitor (interviewer) was assigned inmates to classify. Prior to the interview, the monitor generally reviewed the inmate's institutional and non-institutional records to analyze pertinent data such as the offense, length of sentence, test results, social history, and institutional behavior. After this review, the monitor would meet with the inmate and together they would determine (1) the custody to be recommended and (2) programs and services to fit his needs. Both would then appear before a classification team. This team, consisting of a senior staff member of the PCP (faculty member, Center for Correctional Psychology, University of Alabama), a Board of Corrections representative, and a monitor. They would review the recommendations, insure that all the critical areas had been adequately covered, and make a decision regarding recommendations. Recommendation forms were checked for accuracy and then forwarded to a Classification Board (Board of Corrections personnel) for final approval. If there were disagreements between the classification team and the board that could not be resolved, the board had to justify to the judge why the inmate should not be classified as originally recommended by the PCP. Initially, there were an estimated 800 disagreements between the board and the project recommendations, but most were resolved. By the project's end, only a few individual cases had to be presented to the court for a final decision ("Prisoner Interviews," 1976).

A wide spectrum of persons was employed and utilized to classify the inmates, including lawyers, college professors, psychologists, social workers, and graduate clinical psychology students. This group of PCP personnel was complimented by the classification specialists and psychologists of the Alabama Board of Corrections. The project personnel were predominantly white.

Classification Problems

The implementation of a viable classification plan was considered important, but no matter how good it seemed, any classification procedure could be ineffectual for a predominantly black population unless strategies, procedures, and safeguards were incorporated to obviate cultural, racial, and economic discrepancies between those classifying and those being classified. Ideally, the goal of the classification plan was to eliminate arbitrary, capricious, vague, and discretionary classification decisions.

Therefore, it was necessary to minimize both the very obvious and the subtle ways that factors of sexism, racism, classism, and even incompetence can influence classification. Conversations with others who had previously participated in the classification of prison inmates revealed that those factors could emerge in both decisions and recommendations.

Thus, "gut level feelings," or purely subjective reasons usually offered as a substitute for more tangible evidence in making decisions, were not generally acceptable. The classification of a person as a violence risk required justification based on past or present behavior which indicated that the inmate had a propensity toward violent behavior. Classifying inmate behavior based on objective evidence becomes critical when people from different backgrounds are assigned the awesome responsibility to make decisions affecting the lives of inmates. Rape, for example, may be much more repulsive to some than to others and the strength of this feeling can be manifested through decisions that are made about rapists.

The decisions and recommendations made were to be structured so that they were not arbitrary or unclear. This applied specifically to those recommendations that were made without specifying any time limit or without designating any behavioral objectives. Before the existence of the PCP, an inmate could be assigned a custody with neither specification as to what types of behavior would result in a change of custody for him nor the length of time governing the custody change. In order to curtail this practice, the inmate was to be told how long he would have to remain at a particular custody level and what behavior he would have to demonstrate before he could receive a custody change.

Philosophically, the PCP advocated a positive approach to assigning custody levels rather than adhering to a punishment model. Instead of searching for justifications for keeping an inmate in prison, each prisoner was evaluated for his suitability for community custody. This orientation is different from the traditional view of prison populations.

According to the traditional view, once a person receives a conviction, is given a sentence, and is sent to prison, it is assumed that the individual is incarcerated because he deserves to be incarcerated. This assumption is based on the belief that our system of justice is a fair and unbiased system. Accordingly, an inmate has broken a law of society, has been duly represented by legal counsel, has been fairly tried by peers, and has been fairly sentenced. Recognition of the possible fallacy of this assumption was vital in the classification process.

It was important to realize that just because an inmate was in prison did not mean that he should be there, or because an inmate was in maximum custody did not mean that it was appropriate. Specifically, blacks were more likely to be in prison due to the system of injustice which has assured the victimization of blacks, through plea bargaining, prejudicial police actions, judicial discretion, and other remnants of the system. In fact, it was found from one study of the Alabama prisons that the white inmate received an average sentence of 8.86 years while black inmates received an average sentence of 12.92 years (University of Alabama, 1974).

A classificatory designation then should not be rigidly governed by guilt or innocence nor by the length of a person's sentence. Rather, classification should be based on the determination of the individual's past and present behavior and an assessment of possible future behavior, particularly for reentry into the community.

With this orientation as a foundation when classifying each prisoner, efforts were made to suggest the least restrictive option for that individual. The least restrictive option for one inmate could be release from prison to the community. However, the least restrictive option for another prisoner could be medium or minimum custody. Monitors examined each inmate's past and present behaviors and other variables to determine the appropriateness of his release to the community. Monitors were asked the question, "Do you know of any reasons, based on his behavior and record, why he should not be released to the community?" If there were legitimate reasons to preclude this, he was evaluated for minimum custody. If this were unacceptable, medium custody was considered. This process helped monitors focus their attention on possible reasons why a particular inmate should not be in prison. It became clear that in too many cases the only justification for keeping a person in prison was simply the vengeance of punishment.

The Interview

Every inmate received an individual interview. The purpose of the interview was to gather information to be used to make effective and appropriate recommendations, to isolate concerns of the inmates that were not apparent from the records, and to ascertain any discrepancies or inconsistencies in the inmate's records. The interview was not used to determine whether the inmate was innocent or guilty of his offense.

An accurate and useful classification is enhanced by the cooperation of the inmate. An appropriate climate to nourish this cooperativeness was considered to be highly beneficial. Therefore, the interview was structured to provide for recognition of the rights of the individual, to stimulate inmate input, and to discourage demeaning behaviors by monitors. This was actualized through the use of language the inmate could understand and the practice of social amenities such as introduction of the monitor to the inmate, shaking hands, and saying, "Thank you."

Testing

In order to comply with the mandate of the court to locate and identify those inmates who were psychologically disturbed, mentally retarded, and illiterate, tests were administered. Specifically, each inmate in the prison system was routinely given reading, mathematics, personality, and intelligence tests.

Because there are no known tests free of cultural bias, because the prison population was over 60 percent black, and because testing conditions were not ideal (lack of air conditioning, inadequate lighting, cramped quarters, lack of arm rest and desk facilities, and other deficiencies), extreme caution had to be exercised in interpreting the test results. This sensitivity to tests and test interpretations was influenced by the history of abusive and discriminatory use of testing with minority groups (Barnes, 1972; Williams, 1972). Consequently, test results were not interpreted in absolute terms. The test scores were to be considered in the context of an inmate's total environmental functioning. I.Q. tests, which have received the most criticism for bias against minorities, were used specifically to identify those who were mentally

retarded. However, no inmate was to be labeled retarded solely on the basis of
a test score. Intelligence was to be viewed both in terms of test data and environmental data which minimized probabilities for classifying an inmate as
mentally retarded on the basis of cultural differences or educational deficiencies. The inmate determined to be actually retarded displayed functioning
difficulties both in past and present behavior.

The instruments administered to identify those inmates with serious psychological problems were also closely scrutinized. The Minnesota Multiphasic Personality Inventory (MMPI) was the instrument given to all inmates in the prison
system. Gynther's (1972) research on the MMPI and the discriminatory use of
results with black populations prompted caution in the interpretation of the
results with the black inmates. Where there was evidence on the MMPI of
severe psychopathology, efforts were made to cross-validate this with environmental behavior. In addition, the critical questions and responses that contributed to the pathological profile were verbally presented to the inmate. For
example, some responses given by the inmates to the following MMPI items
were: I feel like there is a tight band about my head (true), people are talking
about me (true), peculiar odors come to me (true), and my sex life is satisfactory (false). Answering the items in one certain direction generally would
contribute to a profile indicating some psychopathology. However, once the
inmate was asked to explain his responses, he could generally produce satisfactory explanations. In many cases, the responses were appropriately classified
as "institutional responses" in that the answers given on the test were a function
of the prison environment. Some inmates did in fact hear guards and others
talking about them, there were very noticeable institutional odors, and the
prison environment was a very tense environment. Of course, a satisfactory
sex life in prison would be highly suspicious. After the responses were discussed
in the interview and the environmental behavior was assessed, some inmates
appeared psychologically different than they were portrayed by the test.

Those inmates whose institutional behavior, pre-institutional behaviors, and
testing results warranted psychological services were so classified and referred
for therapy. The referral of black inmates for psychological services was cau-
tiously recommended.

There has been very little research that specifically addresses the effectiveness of therapy with black inmates. However, the available research on black
populations outside of prison indicate that therapy, as traditionally practiced,
is of questionable value to low income blacks (Banks, 1972; Thomas and Sillen,
1972). This may be due in part to the wide discrepancies between the values
and behaviors of upper and middle class therapists and lower class clients. Since
the prison population is generally drawn from the low income population, it is
reasonable to assume that the same dubious value of traditional therapy applies
to blacks in prison. Therefore, it was recommended that referrals for psychological services cite specific behaviors to be changed so that a more pragmatic
approach could be taken in therapy and more appropriate referrals could be made.

The inmates that were considered too psychologically disturbed for the prison environment were recommended for transfer to a more appropriate institution. Individual, intensive psychological evaluations were recommended when there was some doubt about an inmate's psychological status. Individual evaluations were also suggested for those whose reading level was below the fifth grade.

Correctional Officers' Reports

The reports on inmates from correctional officers were used as current assessments of behavior. However, this procedure proved to be unreliable. In some cases the officers did not know individual inmates and in many cases the evaluation tended to be more subjective than objective. Certainly the lack of training for some corrections officers in behavioral assessment and other related areas was a contributing factor in the subjective reporting. In the main, these reports were not significantly influential in making classification decisions.

Classification Custody Categories

Every inmate was assigned to a custody category. The custody categories represented different sleeping arrangements, different supervision levels, and different degrees of freedom. Maximum custody was the most restrictive. Every institutional custody except minimum required residents to live in single-occupancy cells. Each classification included reliable evidence to justify the custody assigned to an inmate.

Maximum Custody. A condition where the inmate is considered to be dangerous or to pose an extreme threat of violence to self or others. Evidence required for assignment to this category included recent episodes of extreme violence or evidence sufficient to substantiate a reasonable belief that lack of strict supervision will result in extreme violence towards others or self.

Close Custody. The inmate poses a lesser threat of violence to himself or others. Evidence of recent and numerous episodes of violence towards others, recent but not numerous episodes of violence, or recent suicide attempts would justify placement in this category.

Medium. The inmate poses an extreme risk for serious rule infractions, nonviolent criminal offense, and/or escape. Recent escape attempts, recent disciplinaries, or remote episodes of violence toward others would substantiate placement in medium custody.

Minimum. An inmate does not pose an escape risk or violence risk, but may not be psychologically prepared for immediate community custody. Reliable evidence to justify a belief that the person will commit crimes or cannot meet responsibility of community placement is required. Inmate is eligible for passes and furloughs.

Community. The inmate does not pose an escape risk or violence risk and is prepared to meet responsibilities of community placement. Inmate could be on study release or work release, or be housed in a pre-release or other community facility such as a hospital or private residence.

Violent or Dangerous. A very important function of classification was to identify the inmates who were likely to be dangerous or violent. Monahan's (1976) review of the research on predicting violence strongly indicates that even the use of sophisticated testing instruments, authorities in the field of human behavior, and other predictive measures failed to produce reliable results for predicting violent behavior. One finding that emerged consistently from this research on predicting violence was the tendency to overpredict violence. In other words, more people are classified as violent than actually are violent. This tendency was reflected in the court order noting the excessive number of inmates in maximum custody.

In order not to replicate these past mistakes, efforts were made to insure that each inmate was in a custody category that was not more or less than the amount of security he required. The concept of least restrictive alternatives was especially appropriate in this area.

This category received a great deal of attention. Violence in the inmate's background, the nature of his offense, a pattern of violent acts, the recency of the violent acts, the circumstances of the acts, and the nature and number of disciplinaries were all crucial determinants in the classification concerning violence.

Escape Risk. Just as there were no reliable data available that could be used to predict violence, there was also an absence of reliable data that could assist in accurately predicting the escape-prone person. It was finally decided that the best indexes of escape potential for an inmate was actual escape or attempted escape performed recently.

The person was also considered to be an escape risk if there were some factors in his present environment that might provide strong motivation for escape such as a long sentence or a warrant or detainer from another jurisdiction which would mean that he would be eligible for another sentence once the present sentence was completed.

Efforts were made to look for positive behavior and indications that the person was not an escape risk. Nonescape behavior in those situations in which a person could have escaped but did not was considered in making decisions about his escape potential. Also, environmental conditions that might negate escape behavior was also noted, such as close family ties, close parole date, and a clean institutional record.

Disciplinaries

Disciplinaries are written reports of infractions of any institutional rule. The loss of good time or a change of custody were typical punishments given to inmates for disciplinaries. Since there was a general feeling that disciplinaries may have been abused and used capriciously by guards to control inmates, every effort was made to evaluate disciplinaries in terms of those of a relatively serious nature (involving violent acts and potentially violent acts) and those of a less serious nature (insubordination and missing the work gate). The recency of the disciplinaries and the number received by the inmate were also considered. Some of the institutional fighting disciplinaries had to be evaluated in terms of whether it was defensive (protection) or offensive (precipitating the fight).

Educational and Vocational Needs

One of the requirements of the project was to assess both educational and vocational needs. This requirement was accomplished rather easily. Most of the inmates had not finished high school and reading test scores were generally low. With some exceptions, most inmates desired more schooling. The Adult Basic Education (ABE) classes and preparation for the General Equivalency Diploma (GED) were common recommendations. Most inmates also desired some vocational training.

In many instances, a limited exposure to the world of work caused many inmates to be indecisive about future occupational plans. Career counseling, which means that a person would receive interest, vocational, and education testing as well as counseling, was recommended for those inmates.

Case Studies

The following five cases reflect the diverse circumstances surrounding individual inmates. These represent actual classifications recommended by the PCP and illustrates the actualization of the classification process.

Case #1

This was the case of a thirty-one-year-old black male convicted of five counts of robbery. There was no physical harm to any victim. In 1971, he was sentenced to seventy years in prison. His long time was 2042; short time (release date from prison with time deducted for good behavior), 2008; and parole date, 1981.

His current custody was maximum. One escape was recorded in 1972; he was recaptured the same day. Other institutional records revealed two institutional fights (1973 and 1975) and possession of a syringe in 1975.

This inmate was reading on a third grade level; his math level was listed as the fourth grade. He had completed ten years of formal schooling. His interest appeared to be in heavy equipment and automobile repairs. Intelligence test score was in the average range of intelligence and a personality test revealed no serious psychopathology.

Since the inmate had so much time left on his sentence, had previously attempted to escape, and had been involved in some institutional fighting, it was felt that a classification of medium was the most appropriate custody. The inmate was also recommended for ABE classes with preparation for GED enrollment in auto mechanics training. If there were no escape attempts or serious institutional infractions in ninety days, his custody was to become minimum. It was further felt that before the inmate would be ready for the community, educational and vocational skills should be acquired.

Case #2

This thirty-year-old black male was sentenced to prison in 1975 for second degree murder and received thirteen years. His long time was 1988, short time was 1981, and parole eligibility date was in 1979. A review of his records revealed that he had no previous convictions.

The current custody was medium with no escape attempts or disciplinary actions. Despite the fact that the inmate had completed high school, he was reading on a fifth grade level, according to test scores. Other test results revealed a normal range of intelligence and no serious psychological problems.

This inmate had only been in prison for approximately one and one-half years. A first felony offender, the only violence attributed to him had resulted in the present conviction. No negative behaviors were contained in his institutional record. It was felt that a vocational skill would qualify the inmate for community custody. Therefore, it was recommended that the inmate be placed in minimum custody, enrolled in welding school, and after the completion of welding school be placed on work release.

Case #3

This is a thirty-one-year-old black male who was convicted of rape in 1973.

Sentenced to life in prison, his short time was computed as life with a possible parole date listed in 1983. The current offense was the only case of violence in his records. His current custody was medium. There were no disciplinaries or escape attempts recorded. This inmate finished the tenth grade and his test results indicated a third grade reading level and a fourth grade math level. The I.Q. test score was recorded in the low normal range of intelligence. However, he seemed to function adequately in his present environment. There was no psychological test result, but the inmate did reveal that he tended to be depressed, withdrawn, and at times felt very confused about both the present and the future. He did not express an interest in either further occupational or academic education.

Since the inmate had displayed no violence in prison, never had attempted to escape, and had a clean institutional record for three years, it was recommended that his custody be reduced to minimum and that his case be reviewed for work release in six months. It was further recommended that he receive immediate psychological attention for his depression and confusion.

Case #4

This is a twenty-five-year-old black male convicted of rape and night time burglary. Sentenced in 1971 to life in prison, his parole date eligibility was 1981.

His current custody was maximum. No escapes were recorded. Institutional behavior over the five years in prison showed three disciplinaries: 1974—failure to report to assigned job; 1975—possession of contraband; 1976—assaulting an inmate.

This inmate completed high school, but test scores reflected a first grade reading level. His intelligence was recorded as being in the normal range. No individual personality evaluation was given, but environmental behavior reflected no significant psychological problems. His interest in auto mechanics was expressed.

It was recommended that this inmate's custody be reduced to minimum and that he be enrolled in auto mechanic school. After completion of auto mechanics trade, work release was recommended.

Although the inmate had one violent disciplinary registered against him (assaulting another inmate), it was felt that this was not reflective of a pattern of violence. Further, it was the only altercation in a span of almost five years. It was the consensus of the classification team that this was not sufficient to keep him out of a minimum custody. However, a trade was needed to prepare the inmate for the community. It was recommended that the inmate's custody be reduced to minimum. After completion of trade school, he should be considered for work release.

Case #5

A black male, age twenty-eight, had been sentenced in 1969 to seventy-five years for assault with intent to murder and second degree murder. His long time date was 2044, short time date was 2006, and parole date was 1979.

Current custody was medium and no escapes were listed. One disciplinary was recorded in 1970 for "holding up the work squad." The only violence recorded was that connected with the current conviction.

This inmate finished the tenth grade and his reading score was listed as the sixth grade. His I.Q. was recorded in the low normal range of intelligence. His personality test and environmental behavior revealed adequate emotional functioning. Inmate's interest was to be a meat cutter. The inmate was not considered an escape risk or a violence risk, since there had been only one disciplinary in more than six years.

It was recommended that the inmate be placed in a work release center and be allowed to go to a trade school in the community.

These were actual summarized classifications that were agreed upon by the classification team and forwarded to the Classification Board. The final decision by the board has not been received. However, these cases highlight some of the classification recommendations that were made for black inmates in the Alabama PCP.

Conclusion

The prison Classification Project in Alabama was a response to a court order. It began in July 1976 and was virtually complete by Oct. 30, 1976. During that period approximately 4,000 inmates in the Alabama prison system were reclassified.

This classification process was an attempt to evaluate each inmate, as an individual with individual needs and concerns, and recommend programs tailored to these needs. It was an attempt to bring logic to the classification of an inmate and to show some relationship between release from prison and rehabilitative programs.

The effect the project had on the inmates or the correctional work force is unknown. It may be years before the impact of this project can be truly measured and evaluated, and it may be that it can never be accurately assessed.

The project identified new problems. For example, the project classified more people for community custody than there were facilities available. Prior to the classification project, people were assigned to categories and services based upon available space. For community programs, the most suitable were usually selected, rather than other so-called marginal inmates. The project selected many of these inmates, previously identified as marginal, for community programs.

There is no doubt that in this system with its 61 percent black population, many black inmates received rays of hope that would have been missing had they not been part of this experience. There is no doubt that many inmates effected a good con game and some will eventually return to the system. There is also little doubt that some personal biases of the classification team seeped through and affected the objectivity.

The Alabama PCP system was not expected to be a perfect system, nor is classification the ultimate solution to all the discrepancies, irregularities, and biases that exist in the criminal justice system. It is one part of the total process; in Alabama it was an attempt to correct some of the injustices of other components of the system.

One of the significant implications from this project is that in order to rectify some of the injustices that have been perpetrated on the black man, decision makers may have to ask new questions and evaluate the current assumptions that are made about black inmates.

References

"Alabama: Murder Cover-Up Charged." *Southern Coalition on Jails and Prisons Report*, edited by Tony Dunbar. Southern Prison Ministry, July 1975, p. 1.

Banks, William M. "The Black Client and the Helping Professional." In Reginald L. Jones (ed.), *Black Psychology*. New York: Harper and Row, 1972, pp. 205-212.

Barnes, Edward J. "Cultural Retardation of Shortcomings of Assessment Techniques?" In Reginald Jones (ed.), *Black Psychology*. New York: Harper and Row, 1972, pp. 66-76.

Gynther, Malcolm D. "White Norms and Black MMPIs: A Prescription for Discrimination." *Psychological Bulletin* 78 (1972):386-402.

Hippchen, Leonard J. *Correctional Classification and Treatment.* Published for the Correctional Association. Cinncinati, Ohio: W.H. Anderson Co., 1975.

James v. Wallace; Pugh v. Locke, 406F. Supp. 318, M.C. Al., 1976.

Monahan, John. "The Prevention of Violence." In *Community Mental Health and the Criminal Justice System.* New York: Pergamon Press, 1976, pp. 13-34.

"Prisoner Interviews About Done." *Tuscaloosa News,* Dec. 31, 1976, p. 3.

Thomas, Alexander and Samuel Sillen. *Racism and Psychiatry.* New York: Brunner/Mazel Publishers, 1972.

U.S. Department of Justice, Law Enforcement Assistance Administration, National Criminal Justice Information and Statistics Service. *Capital Punishment, 1975.* National Prisoner Statistics Bulletin, NC. SD-NPS-CP-4. Washington, D.C.: Government Printing Office, 1976.

University of Alabama, Center for Correctional Psychology. *Master Plan.* University, Al.: by author, 1974.

Williams, Robert L. "Abuses and Misuses in Testing of Black Children." In Reginald L. Jones (ed.), *Black Psychology.* New York: Harper and Row, 1972, pp. 77-91.

15 Summary

Charles E. Owens and
Jimmy Bell

The task of summarizing the past relationship of the black citizen to criminal justice is not especially difficult. It is abundantly clear that when compared to their percentage representation within the total population, blacks are disproportionately represented at every level in the criminal justice system. There are too many blacks arrested and sentenced and too few in the correctional work force. Only 11 percent of the U.S. population, blacks reflected 35 percent of the federal prisoners and 47 percent of the state prison population. Blacks have experienced double barriers to fairness in the criminal justice system. First, as offenders, blacks are likely to receive the most severe penalty and secondly, as victims, blacks see criminal acts against them go lightly punished or unpunished. Blacks are by no means strangers to crime or to the criminal justice system. Even in the attainment of civil rights, through activities such as sit-ins and marches, blacks had to break the law. The now famous cliche of "when they say justice, they mean 'just-us'" has certainly been appropriate to the black experience.

The task of summarizing the present relationship is much more awesome. It is difficult to realistically evaluate, analyze, and synthesize positive changes in criminal justice operations—especially as these changes relate to the black citizenry. The chore is complicated by the pervasive reality that injustices and irregularities continue to exist in the allocation of justice. One gets the impression that there are rumblings of change and progress, but the rumbles are so transitory and intangible that it is difficult to pinpoint the change. In addition, not everyone feels the rumbles. Some of these rumblings are: that courts are assuming a much more active role in corrections; police are becoming more sensitive to black communities; correctional institutions are becoming more humane; parole officers are becoming service-oriented; and more blacks are being utilized in every area of the criminal justice system.

It is also noticeable that blacks are beginning to take the initiative, organize, and take a leadership role in changing the system. The increasing number of black schools offering criminal justice curriculums to train future criminal justice workers is a testimony to this concept of involvement. Criminal justice organizations structured to address black concerns have increased (lawyers, judges, policemen, counselors, and others). The National Association of Blacks in Criminal Justice is emerging as a central national organization to coordinate the efforts of other organizations focusing on black involvement in criminal justice.

While all these developments are promising, much more needs to be done. Clearly, more research is needed. Blacks have been the most visible offenders, but there is still so very little known about this population. These research efforts must be coordinated and priorities must be established. Of high priority must be the assumption that corrections begins at conception—not at the point of detection. Much more attention must be given to the prevention of crime, both in the home and in the schools.

Finally, we must continue to address the injustices that still remain in criminal justice—the economic enslavement of blacks, the duality of sentencing, and all the vestiges of classism and racism that have lingered on from slavery. Thus, the criminal justice system must be prevented from transcending the inhumane only to become insensitive.

Index

Index

Abernathy, R., 13
Adler, F., 85
Against Our Will: Men, Women and Rape, 78
Alabama, Board of Corrections, 131; Center for Correctional Psychology, University of Alabama, 131; Prison Classification Project, 129–141; prison population, 129–131; prisons, 129–130
Alderson Correctional Institution, 86, 88, 96, 98
American Correctional Association, 13
Amir, M., 76–79, 81–82
Atmore, Holman Brothers, 13

Bail, 28, 38, 51, 54
Banks, T., 4, 37–46
Banks, W., 134
Bard, M., 78
Barlett, D., 28
Barnes, E., 133
Barnes, H., 26, 30, 38, 59
Barnett, S., 4, 25–33
Bayley, D., 26
Becker, H., 54
Bell, D., 42, 44
Bell, J., 5, 6, 113–117, 143–144
"Black Codes," 10
Black colleges and criminal justice programs, 90
Black community, as a colony, 120; causes of crime in, 71, 121–122; coping behavior, 120, 121; crime in, 69, 72; crime control efforts, 69, 73–74, 119; crime control mechanism, 123–127; crime victims assistance program, 21–22; economics, 70; higher education, 116; police relations, 25, 26, 71, 119, 123, 124, 125, 126, 127; powerlessness, 120, 121
Blacks, freed, 8, 9; as lawyers, 29; as judges, 29, 30, 49, 50, 51, 52
Blumer, H., 114

Bontempts, A., 38
Borges, S., 78
Boundary-maintenance, 53, 64
Bowers, W., 79
Briar, S., 26
Bronfenbrenner, U., 19
Brown, H. Rap, 13
Brown, R., 59
Brownfield, A., 69, 71, 73, 113
Brownmiller, S., 78, 80

Campbell, J., 40
Carmichael, S., 13
Carter, D., 80
Center for Correctional Psychology, University of Alabama, 131
Chalmers, D., 11
Chrisman, R., 29, 113
Civil War, 9, 48

Clark, K., 53
Civil War, 9, 48
Clark, K., 53
Classification, problems, 131–133; case studies, 137–140; categories, 135–137; correctional officers' reports, 135; educational, 137; testing, 133–134; vocational, 137
Classism, 47, 48, 53
Cleaver, E., 80
Close custody, 135
Coleman, J., 82
Conklin, J., 72
Correctional Center for Women, 61
Coser, L., 55
Courts, 12, 13, 27, 28, 29, 42, 48, 49, 50, 59, 130
Cressy, D., 82
Crime, types of, 28, 32; interracial, 73
Criminal Justice System and control of, 51, 57–58; definition of, 3, 7; discretion, 4, 37; dual system, 64; higher education, 90, 91, 98, 99, 106, 113, 114, 115, 116; and research, 25

147

Crockett, G., 4, 5, 29, 47–52, 113
Crop lien system, 10. *See also* Share-
    cropping
Curtis, L., 80, 81, 82

Dahrendorf, R., 56
Darnton, J., 26
Darrow, C., 48
Davis, A., 13
Davis, K., 37, 41
Death Penalty, 12, 59, 60
Delaney, P., 26
Dell'Apa, F., 95
Dempsey, Reverend O., 69
Discretion and justice, 4, 5; and deci-
    sion making, 37; judges, 43, 44;
    judicial sentencing, 43; police,
    37, 39, 40; prosecutors, 41, 42;
    and selection of jurors, 42
Dorson, Richard, 3
Douglas, J., 53
Downie, L., 12
Dred Scott Decision, 9

Egerton, J., 39, 113
Eisenberg, T., 90
Elite groups and jutice, 55–56
Elliot, M., 96
Ellis, K., 78
Emancipation Proclamation, 9
Epstein, C., 90
Erikson, K., 54
Evans, P., 5, 75–84
Evers, M., 13
Ex-offenders, 20, 31, 87, 91

Ft. Worth federal institution, 102,
    103, 104, 105, 106
Foster, E., 85–86
French, L., 5, 53–66
Froman, R., 9

Garfinkel, H., 54, 64
Giles, J., 80
Ginzburg, R., 59
Golden, B., 79, 82
Goode, W., 55, 57

Graham, H., 58
Griffin, S., 75, 80
Grossman, B., 40
Gurr, T., 58
Gusfield, J., 55
Gyntner, M., 134

Haley, A., 30
Halsted, D., 26
Hellerstein, W., 30
"Hidden criminality," 57
"Hidden unemployment," 87
Hippchen, L., 130
Hodder, J., 96
Howard University, 90, 91

Inmates, 10, 11, 12, 13, 17, 20, 21,
    25, 30, 31, 32, 55–57, 59–64,
    77, 85, 86, 87, 88, 91, 95, 96,
    98–106, 116, 129–141. *See also*
    Offenders

Jackson, G., 30
Jackson Prison, 13
James v. *Wallace*, 129
Janowitz, M., 38
Jeffrey, C., 19
Jeffrey, I., 19
Johnson, Judge Frank, 129
Jordan, W., 8, 9
Joyner, I., 5, 69–74
Judges, 12, 27, 28, 43–44, 49–52
Judicial system, 49, 64
Jury, 12, 27, 42–43
Juveniles, Juvenile Justice and Delin-
    quency Prevention Act, 19;
    delinquency, 19–20, 72; fami-
    lies, 19–20; number arrested, 72

Kalvin, H., 42
Kaplan, J., 58
King, M. L., 13
Ku Klux Klan, 11, 12
Kuykendall, J., 71

Lawyers, 29, 51, 90, 143
Lee v. *Washington*, 98

Leiberg, L., 88
Lekkerkerker, E., 95–97
Lexington federal institution, 102–106
Liebow, E., 80, 82
Lincoln, C., 9, 10
Lynching, 12

MacCormack, A., 97
Malcolm X, 13, 30
Maximum custody, 135
McArthur, V., 86, 88
McCollum, S., 95, 106
McKay, R., 54, 60
Medium Custody, 135
Meier, 9, 10
Mendelsohn, H., 26
Merton, R., 56
Michael, C., 98
Miller, W., 53
Minimum Custody, 136
Minorities, 25, 27, 29, 32, 38, 42–
    44, 49, 116
Model Penal Code, 43
Model Sentencing Act, 43
Monahan, J., 136
Morgan, E., 13
Myrdal, G., 11

Nagel, S., 27, 28
Nash, J., 12
National Advisory Commission on
    Criminal Justice, 85
National Association of Blacks in
    Criminal Justice, 143
National Commission on the Causes
    and Prevention of Violence, 40
Newman, D., 113
Newman, O., 18
Newton, H., 13
North Carolina, chain gang, 59; cor-
    rectional system, 60, 61; death
    penalty, 59; prisons, 59, 61;
    study of prison population,
    58–64

Offenders, arrested, 17, 20, 38, 57, 69,
    78, 85; dangerous, 44, 136; de-
scriptions of, 17, 18, 72, 78, 81–
    82, 85, 86, 87, 95, 96, 98, 100,
    121, 129; escape risk, 136; in
    jail, 17; in prison, 10, 11, 57,
    60, 61, 63, 85, 95, 96, 98, 129,
    130; racial tension, 130
"One Hundred Years of Lynching," 59
Overby, A., 13, 44, 54
Owens, C. E., 3–15, 129–145
Owens, O. H., 5, 85–92

Palmer, S., 58
Pareto, V., 53
Parker, J., 69, 71, 73
Parker, W., 92, 113
Parole, 57
"Patterns in Forcible Rape," 76
Patterson, P., 87
Piliavin, I., 26
Plantation justice, 7, 8, 9
Platt, A., 114
Police, black officers, 18, 26, 27, 38,
    39, 50, 83; community relations,
    27, 40, 119, 123, 124, 125, 126,
    127; discretionary protection,
    71, 123; treatment of blacks, 11,
    26
Political aspects of justice, 54
Pollack, H., 42
Poor, and the courts, 28, 29, 42, 51;
    and crime, 53–54, 70–71, 87,
    122; and criminal justice, 47, 48,
    49, 86, 114; families, 86; as vic-
    tims, 18
Prell, A., 27
President's Commission on Law En-
    forcement and Administration
    of Justice, 41
Prisons, chain gang, 59; co-corrections,
    102, 103, 104, 105; and convict
    least system, 10; early, 10–11;
    and education programs, 95, 96,
    97, 99, 101, 104, 106; educa-
    tion, adult basic, 99, 106; educa-
    tion, adult secondary, 99, 104,
    106; education, Associate of
    Arts degree, 99; education, Gen-

eral Equivalency Diploma, 99;
education, post-secondary, 99;
education, social, 99, 100, 103,
109; educational staff, 101;
federal, 85, 86, 95, 97, 102–105;
"revolving door," 30, 31; riots,
13, 20, 32, 61; state, 60, 61, 63,
64, 85, 86, 129, 130; vocational
and occupational programs, 88,
90, 95, 97, 99, 100, 104, 111
Probation, 57
Prosecutor, 41, 42
Protests and riots, 13
Pugh v. Locke, 129

Quinney, R., 55, 57, 58, 72

Rader, D., 82
Rape, crisis centers, 82–83; explana-
tions of, 80, 81, 92; interracial,
79, 80, 81; intraracial, 81, 82;
misinformation about, 76, 77,
78; unfounded cases, 77; vic-
tims, 75, 76, 77, 82, 83
Rapist, arrested, 78; executed, 78, 79;
profile, 78, 79
Rasche, C., 98
Reiss, A., 39
Relative justice, 53
Research implications for the future,
31–32
Roberts, A., 95–98
Rose, A., 27
Rudwick, E., 8, 9, 10

Sahiel, J., 45
Sanborn, F., 10, 11
Scheler, M., 56
Schweber-Koren, C., 5, 95–108
Shapiro, B., 30
Sharecropping, 10
Sillen, S., 134
Single parent families, 19, 86
Skolnick, J., 58
Slave, codes, 7; punishment, 8
Smith, A., 42
Smith, R., 80

Social dichotomies, 56
Soledad Brother—Prison Letters of
George Jackson, 30
Stang, D., 45
Steele, J., 28
Steiner, J., 59
Strategies for change, 20
Sutherland, E., 82
Swain v. Alabama, 42
Swan, L. A., 6, 119–127
Sykes, G., 57, 64

Tabb, W., 120
Teeters, N., 26, 30, 38, 59
Terminal Island federal institution,
102, 103, 104, 105, 106
Testing, classification, 130; intelli-
gence, 133; personality, 134
Thomas, A., 134
Townsend v. Burke, 43
"Trail of Tears," 59
Tuskegee Institute, 12

Urban League, 87, 125
U.S. Constitution, 8, 51
U.S. Department of Commerce, 19, 71
U.S. Department of Justice, Drug En-
forcement Administration, 87,
91; Federal Bureau of Investiga-
tion, 17, 20, 26, 38, 58, 63, 69,
77, 78, 79, 85, 91; Federal
Bureau of Prisons, 85, 86, 87,
95, 96, 97, 99–105, 109, 111;
Law Enforcement Assistance
Administration, 12, 17, 18–22,
43, 44, 77, 78, 85, 130
U.S. Department of Labor, 86

Velde, R., 4, 17–23
Victims, description of, 18; rape, 75–
84; survey of, 72–73
Von Hentig, H., 11

Weis, K., 78
Wicker, T., 13
Williams, H., 90
Williams, R., 133

Wolfgang, M., 54, 70
Women, arrest statistics, 85; and
     children, 86; crimes, 61, 62, 63;
     and discrimination, 56, 64; eco-
     nomic profiles, 63, 86; educa-
     tion level, 63, 86, 100; employ-
     ment within criminal justice
     system, 90; prison, 61, 85, 86,
96; in prison, ages, 87; in prison,
     numbers, 60, 61, 85, 95, 96;
     and rape, 75–84; sentences, 87;
     vocational training, 87
Work release, 104
Wyrick, E., 5, 85–92

Zeisel, H., 42

List of Contributors

Taunya Banks
Assistant Professor
Thurgood Marshall School of Law
Texas Southern University
Houston, Texas

Samuel Barnett
Professional Associate
Educational Studies Division
Educational Testing Service
Princeton, New Jersey

George W. Crockett, Jr.
Presiding Judge
The Recorder's Court of the City of Detroit
Detroit, Michigan

Patricia Evans
Bureau Chief
Bureau on the Status of Women
Louisiana Health and Human Resource Administration
Baton Rouge, Louisiana

Laurence French
Assistant Professor
Department of Sociology
Western Carolina University
Cullowhee, North Carolina

Irv Joyner
Director
Community Organization
Criminal Justice and Penal Reform
United Church of Christ
Commission for Racial Justice
New York, New York

Otis Holloway Owens
Associate
Institute of Higher Education
Research and Services
University of Alabama
University, Alabama

C. Schweber-Koren
Doctoral Research Fellow
Research Department
Bureau of Prisons
United States Department of Justice
Washington, DC

L. Alex Swan
Chairman
Department of Sociology
Fisk University
Nashville, Tennessee

Richard W. Velde
Administrator
Law Enforcement Assistance Administration
United State Department of Justice
Washington, DC

Eleanor Saunders Wyrick
Regional EEO Coordinator
Drug Enforcement Administration
United States Department of Justice
Denver, Colorado

About the Editors

Charles E. Owens is an assistant professor in the Center for Correctional Psychology at the University of Alabama. Publications to his credit are *Blacks and the Criminal Justice System*, the Sixth Alabama Symposium on Justice and the Behavioral Sciences, and *Blacks and Criminal Justice: Selected Papers*. He organized and administered conferences that led to the formation of the National Association of Blacks in Criminal Justice (NABCJ) and is presently an executive committee member of that organization. Dr. Owens has worked with inmates in the Wisconsin prison system and assisted in organizing and implementing the Alabama Prison Classification Project, 1976. In addition, he has given numerous lectures on criminal justice issues.

Jimmy Bell is an assistant professor of sociology and director of the criminal justice education program at Jackson State University. He has been active as a consultant with the National Institute of Law Enforcement and Jackson State Police Department. In addition to lecturing nationally on criminal justice matters, he has been actively involved in NABCJ since its inception and is treasurer of that organization.